THE DECATHLON LIFE

THE DECATHLON LIFE

TOOLS FOR CRAFTING YOUR RETIREMENT

BETTY SIEGEL BILL DYKE

**BOOK**LOGIX®

Alpharetta, Georgia

ISBN: 978-1-61005-206-1

Library of Congress Control Number: 2012918346

Printed in the United States of America

∞ This paper meets the requirements of ANSI/NISO Z39.48-1992 (Permanence of Paper)

All scripture quotes taken from the New King James version of the Bible.

All definitions courtesy of Merriam-Webster's Collegiate Dictionary.

Cover photo courtesy of Paul Wendl

DEDICATION

FROM BETTY:

To my husband, Joel, our children and their spouses, and our children's children, who all deserve an Oscar for playing the best supporting family of the year.

FROM BILL:

To Jan, who drives me crazy and keeps me sane in alternate moments, who makes my life fun in spite of the obstacles I put in her way, and who always has been and always will be simply the best.

EPIGRAPH

FULLY COGNIZANT FOR
THE FIRST TIME IN MY LIFE

Dr. Parker Palmer spoke at the Convocation Ceremony for Kennesaw State University's graduating classes in October of 2001. It was a few short weeks after the terrorist attacks on the World Trade Center and the Pentagon. Emotions were still running high.

Dr. Palmer recalled reading about a man emerging from the dust and debris of the World Trade Center on September 11.

"Asked by a policeman if he needed help, the man replied, 'No, I have never been more cognizant in my whole life.'"

Dr. Palmer elaborated: "Cognizant. Fully aware. Thinking. Feeling. In the world with my mind, my heart, my body, my whole being. Aware now of what's important and what isn't important. Valuing people and ideas and possibilities. Fully cognizant for the first time in my life."

We wish this cognizance for you as you craft your Decathlon Life.

CONTENTS

FOREWORD

I have been indelibly marked by the energy and timelessness of competitive athletics for most of my life, and I count this as a blessing. For me, it reached culminating moments when our Atlanta Organizing Committee—which I was privileged to have gathered together and led—won the bid to hold the 1996 Olympic Games, and when I was honored by being chosen to be the President and CEO of the Atlanta Committee for the Olympic Games which would organize and host the event.

These were the "Centennial Olympics" marking the 100th anniversary of the modern Games, and as they always are, the Games themselves were a spectacular demonstration and celebration of talent, commitment, and focus.

It is always inspiring to be in the company of the best of the best. Speaking for me, because of my exposure to the Olympic spirit, I will never be the same and neither will my home town. Together, the athletes who competed in the Games and the tens of thousands of people who helped put them on became more of who they were and exceeded the boundaries of what they thought they could do. The world won't be the same for these folks either.

Dr. Betty Siegel and her husband Joel were "President's Representatives" during the 1996 Olympics, serving as my personal ambassadors to the participants, officials, volunteers, and fans at a particular venue. There were only twenty-eight of these ambassador teams and they were special representatives with a special responsibility: to represent the City of Atlanta, the State of Georgia, and the United States of America to the hundreds of thousands of participants and fans from all over the world. Bill Dyke was an enthusiastic fan, and his son Glenn was part of the Georgia Power volunteer team for the entire course of the Games; they too were participants in making the Centennial Olympics a solid success.

Given that background, it is no accident that *The Decathlon Life* holds a special appeal for me. It is about the Decathlon, of course, but it is really about life, and living life to the fullest. When I was a youngster playing football for the University of Georgia, my father always had a single question for me after the game: "Son, did you play as well as you possibly could?"

This is the question that has guided my life. It also is the question that every Olympian, and particularly every Decathlon competitor, must ask themselves.

It is also the question that only the individual can answer for themselves and the context of both the question and the answer changes constantly.

I am not retired, but I am one of the 74 million members of the "Baby Boom" generation for whom this book has been written. I fully understand the enormous potential represented by these individuals, the experience, talent, and wisdom that, when unleashed, can benefit everyone in every corner of our nation. As Betty and Bill put it, "...people with time on their hands, some with dreams in their hearts. Time and dreams can be potent resources."

This is the generation pondering my guiding question: "Are you playing the game as well as you possibly could?" Members of this group are undergoing major changes in their personal lives while their nation and their society undergo unprecedented structural and economic changes as well. That's the bad news.

The good news is that the retiree has earned the right to be their own boss; they are free to craft the rest of their life as they see fit. They have an opportunity and a challenge to live life to the fullest, to play the game as well as they possibly can, to stretch the limits of who they are truly capable of being.

Perhaps even to craft a Decathlon Life.

I wish you the best in your journey.

Billy Payne

ACKNOWLEDGMENTS

FROM BETTY:

Any book such as this has behind it a long history of indebtedness to the many hands that helped shape it; as the old saying goes, "You never saw a turtle on a post that got there by itself." I would like to single out the following for special acknowledgement:

My parents, Nick and Vera Lentz, early on gave my sister and me extraordinary opportunities to grow in so many ways and inspired us both to dare to dream and do.

My personal and professional mentors, Dr. E.T. York and Dr. Herman Frick inspired others by their example to live a life of integrity, a life devoted to the pursuit of meaning and purpose—the life well-lived; the decathlon life.

I owe a special debt of gratitude to my co-author, Bill Dyke. After I had already given several speeches and written several articles applying the metaphor of the decathlon to leadership, I asked Bill to join me in writing a full book on the idea of the decathlon leader. Immediately, he came up with the brilliant insight to shift focus to the decathlon life—crafting a life after retirement. And so our collaboration was born. With wit, patience, and wisdom he has brought this book from concept to finished product. I have enjoyed working with him every step of the way—thank you, Bill.

FROM BILL:

To Betty and Joel Siegel, whom I have known for only a few years, but for many lifetimes. Like thousands of others before me, I have basked in the wisdom, integrity, and leadership that you bring to the world. I love our synergy.

To Pat Rounds, who runs Betty's office and works miracles on a daily basis. And to Kate Sherman who works for Pat and has been a huge help in our work.

To Jack Labanauskas, who first convinced me I could write and who has become a dear friend. If you, the reader, don't like the book, it's Jack's fault.

To Bryce Emery Sharp, my first real coach, who in my adolescence taught me priceless lessons about hurdling, mathematics, science and character.

To Ahmad Meradji and Kash Mangru at BookLogix who have created a state-of-the-art resource for aspiring self-publishers. Thank you for being truthful and supportive. Live long and prosper.

To Ahmad's exemplary staff, especially Editor Caroline Donahue and Designer Ellina Dent. You saved our bacon more than a few times. If you, the reader, like the book, it's probably because of them.

To cover photographer Paul Wendl and Alpharetta High School coaches Rod Chance and Kirk Alexander. You made it work out beautifully.

To my kids, Lisa and Glenn, and Jan's kids, Chris, Shawna, and Nicole, and their respective spouses and kids of their own, who heard about the book forever, and graciously refrained from rolling their eyes (at least when I was looking), and still may be a little suspicious until they see this in print. I know, through it all, you *wanted* me to write a book and I appreciate your patience.

To Jan. I listened to your ideas and suggestions a lot more than I appeared to, and you were a huge help. As usual.

To John, who left way too soon. We remember.

Finally, to our beautiful cover model Rebecca, and her equally beautiful and understanding sister Emily, and their fabulous mother Suzette who made it all work, thank you.

But a little cartoon light bulb lit up over Bill's head. He had been reading about the demonization of Betty's and his fellow retirees (their entitlements were taking all of our nation's resources!) and felt the media commentators were overstating the danger. He felt the millions of retiring Baby Boomers (born between 1946 and 1964) had gifts aplenty to offer society and collectively should be looked upon as a national resource, not as a burden. The question is how do we tap into that resource? How do we change a negative to a positive? He had not been able to think of a way.

Does the *decathlon* offer a way? Or better yet, for two dedicated meddlers like Betty and Bill—the question became *how* does the decathlon offer a way?

Over the next two hours, Bill worked to link the ten events to life metaphors, and to come up with suggestions to the retirees for ways to design their retirement—no, to *craft* their retirement—no, to craft their *future*. Well, you get the idea. Two hours later, he reported back to Betty with metaphors for five of the events and stories about even more and the discussions and brainstorming began.

So several months and lots of help later, this book is the result. We think it is a different kind of retirement book, for several reasons:

- We call the book "The Decathlon Life," but we don't have a concrete definition for what that means. You will see as you read that we challenge you to define your own Decathlon Life. We just give the craftsman (you) some tools (metaphors) to work with and some instructions and examples of how to use them. What you build is up to you. Think of the possibilities.

- We think you will have a lot of fun with the decathlon events; we were amazed at how valuable the life metaphors turned out to be. Wait until you hear about the high jump, using your imagination, and fifteen-year-old Dick Fosbury; or George Washington and the long jump; or running a metric mile as a celebration. Hold on to your hats.

- We believe that the key to a fulfilling retirement is to focus on the *future*, not the past. This book is all about *beginnings*, and we talk about how that shift in emphasis can change your life. What are you interested in beginning?

- We feel that bottom-up (rather than top-down) innovations and changes work best in our society— maybe in all societies. Regular folks have a lot of good ideas and don't have to depend on a majority vote to implement them. We feel that ordinary people make a huge difference by doing ordinary and extraordinary things in their everyday lives.

- We wrote the book for the individual who is engaged in crafting their own unique life; on the other hand, we have an exceptionally strong suggestion that you enroll an *Advisory Board*, and we wrote a separate chapter to talk very specifically about why and how to do that. It is a must-read. It will challenge you, but you will like the results.

- We try to avoid "best practices" rules and "how-to" instructions. We dislike "Parent/Child" conversations and favor "Peer/Peer" conversations; we hope we convey our sense of respect for who you are. We try to minimize our tendency to meddle.

Ray's "Poor Choice" in Jumping Shoes

Bill was on his high school track team, eventually working his way up to being elected Captain, and he was pretty proud of that. He was a hurdler and sprinter; now and then he would try the long jump (one of the decathlon events) but he was not a very successful jumper.

During his senior year, a football player named Ray decided to join the team and try the long jump. Ray was also a senior, and although he had proven himself to be quite a good football player, this was his first participation with the track team.

Ray brought his own shoes along. Good shoes, heavy shoes, not exactly football shoes, but heavier than track shoes, and, in Bill's judgment, inappropriate for long jumping. Too clunky; the long jump was a sprinter's event, and sprinters and jumpers should wear lightweight track shoes with small, sharp spikes.

Ray may have felt that track shoes were a little too dainty.

In deference to Ray's status as a proven athlete (albeit a novice long jumper), Bill decided not to criticize his shoes on day one. Bill figured that he would let Ray fail miserably as a jumper and then take Ray aside and share his superior wisdom with him and tell him to get rid of the cornball shoes. As Captain, Bill liked to give people a chance to gum things up on their own; it made them more willing to listen to his advice. Besides, Bill was an experienced long jumper, while Ray was a rookie.

Bill never had the chance to have that conversation. Ray had a natural talent as a long jumper and began winning meet after meet; clunky shoes and all. By season's end he was a valuable competitor and made a strong contribution to the team. Bill congratulated Ray and celebrated his success, and kept his mouth shut about the shoes.

(Continued)

xxii

(Continued)

It was a very important discovery for Bill: people who are committed to a goal will almost always be more successful when they are doing things their way than if they are trying to do things the way you think they should.

In the book we may bug you about discovering your strengths and being true to your commitment, but we won't tell you what shoes to wear.

Enough about what we believe. We want you to know more about the exclusive company you are travelling with—the famous Baby Boomers. Read on and find out about your companions.

AUTHOR'S NOTE

A NEW NATIONAL ENERGY POLICY

Demographers tell us that in the United States, more than 10,000 Boomers (members of the "baby boom generation") *per day* are beginning to reach retirement age, and that this will continue over the next nineteen years, totaling somewhat over 74 million folks.

This is an astounding number: 10,000 new people every day, including weekends and holidays. Ten thousand every day will be leaving the corporations, the unions, the small businesses, the airlines, the government agencies, the schools, the restaurants, the military, the dry cleaners, the symphony orchestras. Ten thousand people every day heading out in new directions, beginning to live new lives.

And some critics see it as a problem, as a bad thing, as a burden on our society.

The people who feel that it will be a burden, those who conduct the surveys and write the editorials and read the television teleprompters, are talking about *statistics*, demographics, census data, numbers; they are not talking about real people.

They don't know these people as people. They haven't seen them in action. They have no idea of the personal resources stored up by and available to this flow of 10,000 new "retirees" per day.

These are people with talents and skills that they have been developing and sharpening for the past forty or fifty years. These are people who understand how life works, who have valuable experience in any field you can name and lots you've never heard of. These are people who know how to shoe horses, design rocket engines, and cook gourmet meals. Maybe even the same person.

These are people with time on their hands, some with dreams in their hearts. Time and dreams can be potent resources. The everyday, falling-off-a-log activities of these folks can be a whole new source of national energy. What they have to contribute can be the basis for our new National Energy Policy. What they have to contribute is themselves.

And we wonder how to retain our edge in the world as a country?

Your humble authors propose that we begin to tap into this energy source, this wealth of experience, wisdom and talent. But we say that this energy source has to come to *us*. We can't drill for it, or dig for it, or build insanely expensive equipment to try to harness it.

We have to let this energy source decide how it wants to be tapped. To decide how it wants to take the first step. Actually, to decide in what direction that first step will point them.

And there will be 10,000 *different* first steps every day. That is why the whole national energy thing has such potential, such promise. Everybody is different, which means that every problem, every unique circumstance, can be addressed.

What we need to do as a society is stand back a little while the 10,000 get clear on what they want to do, want to *commit* to do, and then encourage them to design a plan to make that happen.

They may need a little time to decide what they want to do and be, because many of them have spent corporate lifetimes doing whatever the corporation needed done. It may take some soul searching, literally, for them to determine what their personal strengths are, what motivates them, what they can commit to accomplish, what fulfills them. Personal fulfillment may not have been a top priority in their lives up till now, but it will be in the future, because this will be their energy source; this will be what sustains their commitment. Have patience while they work this out.

Perhaps some of the 10,000 won't be physically able to fully participate. Others won't want to, and we must make that okay as well. They have earned the right to make their own decisions. The ranks of the newly energetic won't total the full 10,000 on most days, but who knows? Who can predict these things? When someone is motivated, is energized, who can say they won't find a way to play?

We see this as a movement of individuals. We are reminded of the story of the knights of King Arthur's Round Table; when they collectively saw a vision of the Holy Grail, they all immediately rode off to find it—but each rode in a different direction. Some of the newly motivated Boomers will form organizations and lead movements, but the majority will spend their energy quietly, individually, changing the world one circumstance at a time.

We don't think our fellow Boomers will be exclusive; that is, they won't be contemptuously excluding members of other "generations" from their energetic pursuits. In fact, as we point out in the chapter on Advisory Boards, we see close associations and mutual respect between the Boomers and the Millennials (born approximately between 1982 and 2004) in the future; it just makes sense for both groups. Besides, the Millennials also have lots of energy but lack experience and leverage; collaboration between the two generations could make for a fascinating light show.

We need to let our compatriots know that it is okay for them to get off the couch, okay for them to envision a future after retirement, okay for them to discover what fulfills and motivates them, okay for them to dream and to pursue those dreams. We may never know what miracles they accomplish as they manifest those dreams, but the people around them will.

So your authors thought we might put some ideas together, might suggest some life metaphors, derived from the decathlon, to amuse and enlighten and perhaps even inspire the Boomers on their journey.

> ### Holy Moses!
>
> In the Christian Old Testament, the Jewish Torah and the Islamic Koran, the prophet Moses was a shepherd when he was called by God to confront the Pharaoh, the ruler of Egypt, and lead the Jews out of slavery and across the Sinai Desert to their "Promised Land."
>
> Moses was 80 years old at the time.
>
> Leading a group of rebellious people, former slaves at that, across a hostile desert is not for kids. Maturity is a definite plus. But the group ultimately managed to hang together off and on as a nation for more than a thousand years and as a distinct and proud people for a total of 3,500 years (and counting).
>
> For various reasons things did not go well on the journey and the group spent the next forty years in the desert. Moses was allowed to see the Promised Land but was not allowed to enter; he died on Mount Nebo in about 1450 BC.
>
> He was 120 years old when he died.
>
> Think about it.

CHAPTER 1

THE DECATHLON METHODOLOGY

You, the reader, may be much more organized and alert than your two authors are, but for us, we like some "Learning Aids" and "Memory Joggers." To that end, we have included a methodology for remembering what we talk about in our book. The methodology is based on a series of track and field events, including athletic contests that have existed for 2,500 years. No, your authors haven't been around all that time, but several of the events have, and we figure that anything that has lasted for two and a half millennia must have something going for it.

Our methodology, of course, is built around the ten events of the modern decathlon. In the upcoming chapters of the book we develop metaphors from these events; metaphors which we feel will be helpful as you deal with the challenges and opportunities of crafting your future. These metaphors are designed to be tools and resources for you to use in your journey.

As a beginning, this chapter will introduce the events and give you a preview of the metaphors.

History's Greatest Athletic Event

The Olympic Decathlon is considered to be the greatest all-around athletic competition in the world, featuring athletes who have endured rigorous qualifying rounds to win a chance to participate in the finals. There is something profound about being able to trace the roots of your event back to what is, arguably, the oldest recorded athletic competition of all time. In recognition of the esteem and high regard with which the Olympic Decathlon is held, the winner of the competition is given the unofficial title of "The World's Greatest Athlete."

The Decathlon consists of ten events:

- Three "jumps:" High Jump, Long Jump, and Pole Vault.
- Three "throws:" Shot Put, Discus Throw, and Javelin Throw.
- Four "runs:" 100 Meters, 400 Meters, 1500 Meters, and 110 Meter Hurdles.

If you grew up around track and field meets, as Bill did, these events are old hat, but just in case, as we come to each event in the book, we will explain how each works and even a little of its history.

You will find that no event is like another event. Even though some may require similar skills and talents, they are all quite unique. This quality is why the decathlon is so interesting; in this day of specialization, the decathlete (yes, they have their own unique name) must master a plethora of athletic skills: strength, speed, gymnastic grace, endurance, balance, even instinct. Some of these reflect parallel skills in life as well as in sport.

Why Pick the Decathlon?

In using the ten events of the decathlon to develop resources for crafting your future, we are able to offer you a variety of choices. With 10,000 new journeys beginning every day, there are no "best practices," no "one size fits all" to fall back on, and this is probably a good thing. The Decathlon Life is written upon a clean slate; no two journeys will be identical. The metaphors developed from the decathlon events are submitted to you for your own individual consideration; we hope you will find one or more to be useful. It will please us if you feel we have aided you in your journey.

The ten events provide ten metaphors for assembling your plan, for charting your own journey, for crafting your Decathlon Life. Ten seems to be a reasonable number; it provides a variety of choices without being overwhelming.

Some metaphors apply at different times in your journey (choosing a *commitment* and focusing on the *start* come up front; the *celebration* fits in at the end) but not all. Our suggestion is that you begin with choosing a commitment (this is what everything else is built on) and then pick one or two or three more that you like and concentrate on those.

There are some that are hard work, but you may be ready for hard work. Others are more peripheral and may be interesting to us, but not to you. Pick and choose what works for you and remember that what looks like a waste of time today might be fascinating and just what turns you on six months from now.

Here is a preview of each event and the metaphors that they bring:

Metaphors for the Decathlon Life

400 Meters:

Commitment

As the most demanding event of the decathlon, the 400 meters serves as a perfect metaphor for commitment, starting with choosing what you can be truly committed to accomplish. When you commit, you are making the choice to engage, to get on the playing field. What accomplishment is important enough to you to enable you to sustain this engagement? Crafting your Decathlon Life, focusing on the future,  envisioning what you want to achieve may be tough and the 400 can be an inspiration. Everything else in the Decathlon Life flows from choosing your commitment, like a swift stream from a tiny spring.

100 Meter Dash:

Power Start

The 100 meter dash provides a metaphor for crafting a power start for your journey. As the craftsman, you design the first stages of manifesting your vision, increasing your chances for producing early results that motivate both you and your team. You avoid starting two or three projects at once; the eagle that chases two rabbits catches neither. The 100 meters is a  metaphor for preparation; for planning; for attention to detail; for being alert, energized, and focused when the starting gun goes off. The start is the time to feel the incredible power of beginnings.

Discus:

Committed Beginner

How can we become beginners after a lifetime of experience? Your dreams may take you into new territory. The discus teaches us that some things may not be as simple as they appear, and it doubles as a metaphor for the Decathlon Life participant being willing to ask for coaching and for learning something new. We all have seen times when we gained from being a committed beginner in a particular domain, and the discus metaphor can be of great  benefit to us in our continuing education. A new sense of accomplishment and a new skill may be in your future.

Long Jump:

Expanding Boundaries

We will undoubtedly come up against our boundaries, our stopping points, when we begin crafting our Decathlon Life. The Long Jump can be a metaphor for expanding boundaries that impeded you in the past. You are living into the future now; new possibilities are the rule, not the exception. One of the ancient Olympic events and a battlefield skill, the long jump metaphor can give you the extra motivational punch to achieve your goals and help others achieve theirs.

Shot Put:

Personal Strengths

While champion shot put athletes exhibit agility and timing, it is the event that most requires the decathlete to generate maximum physical strength. Metaphorically, here is the chance for you to reflect on your own personal strengths, on what makes you unique, on the experience and wisdom you have accumulated over the years, and on the contribution to the future of the planet that you alone can make. The shot

put metaphor encourages and enables you to choose to be more of who you have always been and who you have the power to become.

110 Meter Hurdles:

Instinct and Intuition

The 110 meter hurdles is an instinctive event. You can't think and hurdle at the same time. In the Decathlon Life, the 110 hurdles event is a metaphor for trusting your instinct, developing your intuition, learning to use your inner voice, going with your "gut." The ancient Greeks recognized three "centers" of human existence; the Mind (thinking), Heart (feeling), and Gut (instinct). The 110 hurdles metaphor enables you to open up  this third center and experience its power. You may not know what you've been missing.

High Jump:

Imagination

Things always change, plans need revising. Sometimes we have to change directions, take a different approach, be creative, and use our imagination. The high jump is a metaphor for being flexible and innovative when we craft our Decathlon Life. We want to keep light on our feet. Sometimes we will even choose to go against the grain of "looking good." The high jump metaphor opens our possibilities and keeps us looking for something new.

Javelin:

Leverage

The javelin is the decathlon's *longest* event: competitors throw a two pound spear close to 300 feet, or the length of a football field. The javelin throw is a metaphor for leverage, for expanding your range, for extending your influence and impact in the world, and for becoming more of who you can be. In ancient times, javelin throwers sought a prominent place to improve their vision and increase their leverage; the javelin metaphor challenges

us to utilize the prominence available to all of us to move the world forward.

Pole Vault:

Perspective and Inspiration

The pole vault is the decathlon's *highest* event, with athletes vaulting up to reach the height of a two-story building. The pole vault event is a metaphor for changing your perspective, for *rising above* the mundane and the ordinary; for entering the domain of inspiration; for converting horizontal energy into vertical energy; for connecting with something bigger than we are. Our Decathlon Life, like the vaulter,

can raise us and those around us to new heights.

1500 Meters:

Celebration

As the last event on the two-day decathlon schedule, the 1500 meters is a metaphor for celebration, for experiencing the joy of having competed with friends, not enemies; for having shared the exhilaration of being engaged; for having been on the playing field doing what you do best with people you respect and even love. The 1500 meters metaphor is about stopping and reflecting: didn't we create a great future?

Decathletes and the Decathlon Life

Just like you, the young decathlon athletes have spent their lives getting to this point. If they have qualified for Olympic competition they are at the peak of their game, but you may be too. You may be afraid that you have peaked and are declining, but in many cases you are on the cusp of finding out what you came here for.

It is a culminating period for the decathletes as they face the two days of intense competition. Imagine yourself addressing the collected decathlon competitors and asking: How do you want to craft your future? How do you effectively use your resources and your energy? How do you keep your performance level high? *Who are you really capable of being?*

These, of course, are the same questions you will be asking yourself as you engage in the Decathlon Life. This is why the metaphors work.

THE 400 METERS

CHAPTER 2

THE 400 METERS

Commitment

Welcome!

So you are considering engaging in the Decathlon Life. Welcome! We're glad you're here!

You might be wondering about the details, about why "commitment" is first, about why it is so important to the Decathlon Life. We'll get to that in this chapter, but first things first. Let's talk about the 400 Meters!

The 400 meters can be considered—with the possible exception of the marathon—the most difficult running event in modern track and field competition. It is a race that takes the participants once around the oval track, approximately a quarter of a mile, and is run at sprinter speed. More than one runner has heard the statement, "The 400 is for horses, not human beings."

The 1968 Summer Olympic Games were held in Mexico City, Mexico. Never before had an athletic event of this size been held at such a high altitude (over 7,000 feet above sea level), where oxygen deprivation can be a real problem. U.S. Olympian Lee Evans, running in the rarified atmosphere, set a new world record for the 400 meters, but he was visibly struggling at the end of the race. When asked by reporters what was going through his mind during the last few meters, he sighed and said "I was just trying to survive."

No one chooses to compete in the 400 meters lightly. You may decide to take up a less demanding activity—perhaps white water kayaking, skydiving, or fire walking—with more carefree abandon, but running the 400 will take everything you are and ever hope to be.

It will take courage. It will take engagement. It will take *commitment*. The 400 meters runner, if they intend to compete with others, must commit themselves to a regimen of exhausting training. The 400 requires a daunting mix of speed, strength, and stamina.

In much the same spirit, choosing to live a Decathlon Life begins with making a commitment. We are not talking about a New Year's Resolution (you know how those turn out). Just as the 400 meters runner knows that they cannot build a successful career on good intentions, the Decathlon Life participant needs to get serious about commitment.

Resistance

How people might express their resistance to commitment:

- No one else is telling me I have to commit to something. I like to keep my options open. I'm leery of making commitments.

- I tried getting involved with something to keep me busy, but it turned out not to be what I thought it was and I gave it up. I'm not sure I want to try anything else for a while. This sounds like a lot of work, and I just retired from working. Why would I want to do something that sounds like work?

- Are you suggesting I start a whole new career?

- I'm not as young as I used to be. I get tired easily. I don't feel very energetic. It's probably not my cup of tea.

- I don't have the support team, the key contacts, the business associates I used to have. I'm pretty much on my own now. How could I start over? Who would I get to help me?

In *Illusions*, Richard Bach said "Argue for your limitations, and sure enough, they're yours." When you can see that the statements above (and thousands of others just like them) are just expressions of resistance, you can choose to push past the resistance and craft a new future, a new life; a life based on committing to something, maybe even something bigger than you are. You might even call it a Decathlon Life.

But for most of us, making commitments has never been something we do every day, and now we're *retired*, for Pete's sake! Give us a break!

So let's begin with reasons we would want to overcome our resistances, reasons we would want to make a commitment.

Let's look at the life of a decathlete.

The Improbable Decathlete

No one becomes a decathlon athlete because someone holds a gun to their head. No one sees it as a career path; as a soft way to easy riches. Chances are, their active life as a decathlete is over before they reach forty, and maybe long before. Very few ever earn six-figure incomes. All in all, there are lots easier ways to make a living.

Decathletes choose to be decathletes because of the challenge, because they love living for maximum performance, because they are fulfilled by becoming the best at what they are already very good at. A sports team once had a sign above their locker room door reading "Today is for the Championship." They recognized that when you live life to the fullest, *every* day is an important step toward the ultimate championship—whatever that championship might be. The team members approached their schedule of tasks for the day as committed as if they were playing in the championship game. Can you see how effective that could be?

Decathletes are personally fulfilled by contributing the wondrous gift they have been given, the gift of exceptional athletic skills and talents. They are the best of the best; they each have a very visible, very unique "piece" to place into the grand mosaic called "life."

Most of us mere mortals have more modest gifts, less likely to qualify us for an appearance with Oprah, but they are gifts nonetheless. We have one grand opportunity in equal measure with the most talented decathlete: the opportunity to be the most of who we really are.

When it comes to choosing a commitment—choosing what to be committed to accomplishing—decathletes have limited choices. The ten decathlon events are probably not going to change very soon; after all, four of them have been around for 2,500 years.

We, on the other hand, have an absolutely unlimited choice of paths to take, of challenges to accept. Well, perhaps becoming an astronaut or a prima ballerina is a bit of a stretch at our age, but you get the point.

But let's get back to that idea of what we have in common with decathletes, that opportunity to be the most of who we really are. What does that look like in real life?

The Decathlete: Surpassing Your Previous Best

Decathlon competitors don't just show up at the trials every year or so, they commit their time, their energy and their attention all year long to give themselves the maximum chance to achieve their ultimate goal: a better performance than their previous best.

Decathlon competition is unique. There is a points table for each event, showing the points awarded for a particular level of performance. For the 400 meters, for example, a portion of the table might show:

Event Time (seconds)	Points
48.0	902
47.0	951
46.0	1001

As the athletes complete each of the ten events their performances are converted into points which are then added to the running total tabulated for each participant. At the end of the competition the athlete with the highest cumulative number of points for all ten events is declared the winner and the medals are distributed. Throughout the days of competition, the athletes are competing, not so much against each other, as against themselves;

striving to surpass their previous best performances, to break their own individual event records, to accumulate a new personal record total of points.

When you choose what you will commit to, make your goal to surpass your previous best. If you are committed to traveling your country or your world, make the trips more memorable or more meaningful, or both. If you are committed to improving your local school system, make a plan that, when implemented, results in measurable and sustainable gains. Extend your boundaries—today is for the championship.

The good news is that there are no right answers as to what you "should" commit to accomplishing. You are on your own. Here is your perfect chance to have your own way. No other person has a right to try to interfere with your choice. The vote will ultimately be one to nothing. It is probably best to avoid the prima ballerina thing, however.

The bad news is that there are no right answers as to what you "should" commit to accomplishing. You have to choose. No one can choose for you, and different choices will lead to different journeys. You are taking the first and, arguably, the most important step in crafting your future. Changing your mind, however, is permitted, as we will point out in a moment.

How Will I Measure Success? What Is My End Game?

Bill was once serving as a consultant to a small computer software company as the company was finalizing the design of a development project with a major railroad. It was a two–step project: if the initial design phase (which would bring the software company several hundred thousand dollars in revenue) proved to be successful, the railroad would commit to the larger project worth additional millions of dollars. Bill was meeting with the top representatives of the software company and an executive of the railroad at a conference center in California to finalize the design and sign the contract.

Bill had not been involved in the prior negotiations leading up to this meeting so he was doing more listening than talking. Everything seemed to be going well and the session was winding down when Bill turned to the railroad executive and asked a single question:

> What is your criterion for judging the initial, trial phase to be successful? What evidence will you be looking for, what data will you need, to commit the railroad to the full-scale project? How will you define success?

It was not a profound question, but it was the right question. The room grew quiet. No one on either side of the table had an answer. The executive spoke first: "Good question. I guess we need to develop an answer for that right away."

Lewis Carroll, of *Alice in Wonderland* fame, said, "If you don't know where you are going, any road will get you there."

You can see the advantage of having a definition of success: it sharpens your thinking and gives you a way to minimize or eliminate those activities that don't directly contribute to achieving your commitment. We imply that it is "measurable" success, but if your commitment is to developing a more fulfilling relationship with your spouse, most of the evidence of success is going to be anecdotal. This doesn't detract from the value of achieving the results, and the stories you tell could make you the envy of your friends.

What if I Change What I Am Committed To?

If you get deep into your planning, or even into the pursuit of your committed result, and decide to change things—even *major* things—good for you! Give yourself a hearty pat on the back!

Changing your mind doesn't mean you are indecisive, or in denial—it means you are *engaged*. You are paying attention. You may be getting to know more about your group, or your community, or your country. You definitely will be getting to know more about yourself.

Betty Changes Her Major – And Her Life

From Betty:

One of my first college classes was chemistry. It was a large class in a large room and I was the only female there.

Not a good sign.

The professor walked in, scanned the classroom and his eyes settled on me.

"What are you doing here?" he boomed.

In a much less authoritative voice I answered, "I'm studying to be a doctor."

"The only place for women in medicine is as nurses and attendants!" he retorted. That was the end of my medical career.

I immediately went to the administrative office and changed my major. I concentrated on psychology and sociology, expanded that to pursue a career in education and over the years earned a PhD in Early Childhood Education. I had excellent mentors and coaches and loved my new life path.

I think under different circumstances I could have become a doctor. And I think I would have made a good doctor and would have blazed at least a little trail.

(Continued)

(Continued)

But I don't think I would have had the impact as a doctor that I had when I became the first female Dean at the University of Florida, or the first female President of a college in the University System of Georgia. I'm really not sorry that my chemistry professor pushed me in a different direction.

I'm sure he thought he was doing me a favor, and in fact he gave me a gift. He didn't change my commitment; he just nudged me to change what I was committed to.

And after all, as Yogi Berra once noted, "If you come to a fork in the road, take it."

Betty took what seemed like an insurmountable barrier and turned it into a springboard; a motivation to craft a life of pioneering breakthroughs and accomplishments.

Commitment is like that. When you are fully committed to producing a specified result, you have to evaluate the resources that are available to you, and the most important of those resources is *you*. As you get to know yourself better, it is acceptable to change your objective. Just remember that your goal is to surpass your previous best. The journey is at least as important—and rewarding—as reaching the goal.

Searching for You

People have written books and delivered seminars and built careers out of helping people find out who they are. We aren't going to recommend books or seminars, but if you choose to engage in that kind of search to augment your Decathlon Life commitment, we respect your choice and your freedom.

We feel it is vitally important, however, for you to get some insight into what you want and what you bring. In that light, we offer a short exercise that you might try that has been useful to us. At least the price is right: free.

Here is how it goes:

- Get a pad of paper and start writing about who you are, what your strengths are, what your talents are, what you like, what you don't like, what your values are, what motivates you, what you could commit to, what you think is bull feathers, what upsets you, what attracts you, what fulfills you, what has worked for you, what hasn't worked for you, what you have enjoyed doing, what you despise doing, what about you surprised you, what about you encouraged you, what about you others liked, what about you others didn't like, on and on and on. Don't edit it or try to make it make sense. Write page after page after page, just as it comes to you. Try to be factual; keep judgments out of it. Just call it like you see it.

Now put it away for a day.

- Sit down with what you wrote and look for trends, for patterns, for evidence. Don't judge what you find, just report it. Now write *one page* summarizing what you found.

(Continued)

(Continued)

Put it away for a day.

- Sit down with the one page and condense it into one paragraph: Who you are.

Put it away for a day.

- Condense the paragraph to one sentence.

- Condense the sentence to three words.

- Keep these words in mind as you search for what you want to commit to.

Contribution

Not everybody can be the king. Some people will be King Arthur or Joan of Arc, some will be Merlin, some will be Lancelot; most will just be who they are and do what they do and perhaps be called upon to be the Hero Next Door.

But life is designed to be fulfilling at any level on the social hierarchy scale. We contribute who we are, we do what we do best and it fulfills us. Yes, it can be a different world for the king and for Merlin, but it can be a different world for everyone if we but allow it.

We feel that the concept of contribution is a fairly simple model:

- We all have something, some talent, some personal strength that defines "what we do best." There may be more than one, but there are not many, unless our talent is "being flexible and multi-talented."

- When we are consistently doing what we do best, we get a sense of personal fulfillment. This has been defined as "doing what you love," or "following your bliss." This is discussed in more depth in the section

23

"Personal Fulfillment and Team Fulfillment" in the chapter entitled "Your Advisory Board."

- When we are doing what fulfills us, we don't need a lot of outside motivation. We tend to work long hours without realizing that the time has passed; we are doing what we do because we want to. This is sometimes defined as "enlightened self-interest." We don't do what we do because we will get a tote bag at Thanksgiving; we do it because it is what we do best.

- In the same way, we don't have problems with sustainability over periods of time; we don't look for reasons to leave; we don't have to be prodded out of bed in the morning. We don't spend our lives dreaming about vacations, holidays and retirement. We can keep going when unmotivated people quit.

- Our life can become even more fulfilling when we get a sense that what we are engaged in has meaning, has value in our world. When all is said and done, we can define "meaning" and "value" however we want.

And this becomes what we contribute to the world. We contribute our talents, our strengths, our piece of the mosaic. We give of who we are.

This is what you ultimately will want to commit to contributing.

THE 100 METER DASH

CHAPTER 3

THE 100 METER DASH

Power Start

Getting Started

Now you have made a choice; you know what you are committed to, at least for the first lap or two, and you're not afraid to decide to change your mind.

But you still aren't exactly sure where or how to begin. It looks a little new and maybe unfamiliar; you wish you had a clearer picture of an elegant way, or at least a graceful way, to get started.

Let's look at how important a start can be. Let's look at the 100 Meter Dash!

The 100 meter dash is the shortest event in outdoor track and field competition. Olympic Games 100 meters competitors finish the race in ten seconds or less. The winner is usually deemed to be "the world's fastest human."

The 100 meters is the race where the winning performance is the most profoundly determined by the start. Participants spend long hours developing the first eight or ten steps of their race. Their intention is to come out of their starting blocks with such explosiveness and power that they achieve an early lead; a lead their competitors will be unable to overcome. If you win the start, your chances of winning the race are very good.

On the other hand, an explosive start takes an awful lot of energy. From a crouching start, the athlete is burning energy at a prodigious pace to get up to full sprinting speed.

There is a lesson here for those choosing to engage in the Decathlon Life. Put in the time and thought required to be prepared for the start, work hard to create an early momentum, but also understand that during the beginning of your endeavor you are expending a great deal of energy for a relatively small return. There is nothing wrong with that, it's just the nature of the start.

The purists among our readers are probably wondering why the start is the second metaphor in our description of the Decathlon Life, and not the first, where we have placed commitment. The two are interdependent and closely linked, almost like dual stars orbiting each other—the start without a commitment is hollow and unsustainable, while the commitment without the start is just daydreaming.

The Start Is a Beginning

The Start is a beginning and we are very big on beginnings. Human beings remember and celebrate beginnings; beginnings generate energy, elevate emotions and reveal new possibilities. Beginnings send a signal to the universe that we are not done yet.

They send the same signal to us.

Preparation

But we place the commitment first because it forces us to focus on the ultimate results, not the beginning—the achieving of the goal, the breaking of the tape. Once we confirm our commitment to the successful finish, we can begin our preparation for the start. And speaking of that preparation, we have some suggestions.

First, develop a plan for the activities of the start. What will you need to do to get started in your endeavor? What specific tasks have to precede everything else? It doesn't have to be a long or detailed plan—the most effective military leaders will say a battle plan is only good until the first shot is fired—but the work you will do putting a start plan together will sharpen your mind. Remember, this is only the first eight or ten steps of the race.

Your start plan is not your long-term plan. As events unfold and your start leads to a better understanding of the challenges and opportunities you face, you can begin to develop a long-term plan to achieve your committed result. What you want to accomplish with your start plan is an early but measurable result, something that you can point to as a sign of progress, a sign of early momentum.

Early Results

Bill was with IBM in Atlanta, Georgia during the early days of mainframe computers, when only the largest of organizations could afford to invest in automating large portions of their work. One of the businesses on the leading edge of computerization in those days was Southern Railway (Now Norfolk Southern), a large railroad system with headquarters in Richmond, Virginia and Atlanta. Their computer development effort was headed by Jack Jones, a man of exceptional intellect, management skills, and common sense.

Most corporate executives (the people who signed the paychecks) had to depend on people like Jack to manage the computerization of their organizations; the complex implementation projects went on for years and cost millions of dollars; success was not guaranteed until the projects were completed. The executives lost a lot of sleep.

Jack Jones solved the problem for Southern Railway with a brilliant technique: when he designed a long, complex project, he arranged the work so that he could demonstrate

(Continued)

(Continued)

a small success within the first few months, and additional successes, which began to produce real cost savings, every three to six months thereafter. People working on the project were more enthusiastic, the other railroad employees were more inclined to be optimistic and cooperative, and the corporate executives slept more soundly.

Jack recognized the advantages of a power start and showing early results.

Along with planning, we recommend engaging in some research. Unless you are already an acknowledged expert in your chosen endeavor, you probably are going to benefit by diligently scouting out the new territory.

Others have done what you are starting to do; what has been their experience? Are there books or web sites dealing with your new passion? How can you learn from the experiences of others, without repeating their mistakes? As you delve more deeply into the details of your new endeavor, you may redirect your emphasis a bit, or even a lot. This is good; you are engaged. Remember, at the start, you are expending a disproportionate amount of energy for a relatively meager increase in velocity, but like a competitor in the 100 meters, as you gain momentum, this will reverse and you will begin to cruise.

An additional recommendation is to begin early the task of enrolling the members of your Advisory Board. We have not introduced the details of a enrolling a board of advisors at this point, but we cannot emphasize enough the importance of establishing a strong group of colleagues to guide and assist you. These are the people who agree to be your volunteer advisors as you begin to craft your Decathlon Life. They can be invaluable in helping you get off to a good start.

Finally, learning from the feedback you receive during your start is the key to long term success. Keep your eyes open in the early stages of crafting your Decathlon Life and draw upon the experience of your years in interpreting and evaluating what you see. Remember that you are honing and developing your skill as a craftsman as you go. Watch the momentum build.

Bill's Bad Start and Life Lesson

From Bill:

My first management job came when I was twenty-seven-years-old, but still wet behind the ears. I was an engineer in Procter and Gamble's headquarters in Cincinnati when I was promoted to be a Shift Foreman in P&G's Chicago manufacturing plant, one of the largest plants in the company. I was going to be working in the "Tide Tower," the most important department in the entire facility. We produced 50,000 pounds of laundry detergent every hour, around the clock, with only about fifteen people on each shift. The jobs in the Tower were the most complex and best paying jobs in the plant and the crews were absolutely top notch.

So I was going to make my crew better.

These were all just regular folks, probably in their forties and fifties; just everyday people—regular, everyday, exceptionally talented people who were at the top of their game.

But now I had arrived, and I was going to make them better.

I had staked my life on being the best, and it had worked out pretty good so far, so I was about to apply my life philosophy to managing people. The other two shift foremen were older guys who had been promoted up from the ranks; I was sure I could outshine them. I began to instruct my crew on how they could improve.

(Continued)

31

(Continued)

Thank goodness they were gentle.

Jack, the lead Tower operator, was a big, good natured guy in his late fifties. We had some great discussions about how the high-tech detergent-making process worked, but our conversations always seemed to get back around to my management style. He laughingly grabbed me around the head one night with his big hairy arm and said "You know, when a baseball team isn't winning, they don't fire the team, they fire the manager!" He thought that was hilarious; me, not so much.

Chas was the youngest and probably the most intellectual guy on the crew. He ran the chemical mixing process; his skill (and he was very good) determined whether or not we met our critical quality measurements. A mistake on his part could cost thousands of dollars in a hurry. Actually, that was true of everyone on the crew; they had the jobs they had because they were the best; they just didn't make mistakes.

About four a.m. one quiet Chicago morning, Chas and I were outdoors on the ninth floor catwalk of the tower, just talking, leaning over the low hand rail, waiting for the cleanup crew to finish a brand changeover. Chas didn't have Jack's sense of humor; he was quieter, less talkative, and chose his words before he spoke. He had been commenting on how tough I was being in managing the crew. I was arguing that I just wanted them to be the best.

In a casual tone, looking at the empty parking lot a hundred feet below, Chas said "You know, for $300 one of these guys could have you taken out."

I knew what "taken out" meant. After all, this was Chicago.

I knew it was not a real threat. Chas didn't mean it that way. Like the farmer who hit the mule in the head with a two-by-four, Chas was just getting my attention.

(Continued)

> *(Continued)*
>
> But again, it *was* Chicago.
>
> I saw the light. I made some quick and substantial changes. I set my sights on learning from my crew instead of trying to teach them what they already knew (better than I did), and they embraced my new management style enthusiastically.
>
> And magically, they did get better, all on their own, and made me look good (to the uninitiated) by doing it.
>
> Even a bad start can be overcome. What I learned from that exceptional crew about managing people has made my life and the lives of those around me a lot more pleasant.

One last note: when you start your Decathlon Life journey, you are establishing a moment in time, a memory that you can refer to when you need to bolster your commitment. On this day, by this action, you drove a stake in the ground. Here the journey began. You declared that you are a player, you are in the game, and you are taking responsibility for crafting your future. You are beginning your engagement in the Decathlon Life.

Tradition - The Daruma

 In Japan, the start of a new venture is often marked by painting in one eye of a Daruma, a papier-mâché doll that is a sort of goodluck charm. The dolls are sold with both eyes blank; tradition says that painting in one eye at the beginning of a project brings the Daruma's spirit to life so that it can help you achieve your goals.

When you meet your objective, tradition calls for you to paint in the other eye, thus granting full expression to the spirit of the Daruma as a reward for its service.

CHAPTER 4

COMPETITION, COMPETING, AND EXCEEDING OUR BEST

There are those who are repelled by the whole concept of sporting events, of athletic contests, of games where one participant wins and all of the others "lose." Robert Bly, writing in *Iron John*, describes some people as "addicted to harmony."[1]

Yes, athletic contests, including the events of the decathlon, are games where there are winners and losers, and most participants in these contests would be bored to death if you didn't keep score. But there is more to the story.

The early derivation of the word "compete" was from the Latin *competere*, meaning "to seek, to come together, to agree, to be suitable." To compete originally meant to come together, agree and, arguably, work together toward a common goal.

We like this way of describing competition. The decathlon brings together the greatest of the great athletes of the world, and the events are about these athletes performing at their best and even beyond their best, and certainly are not just about who wins and who loses. All of the competing athletes are, in fact, working together toward the common goal of exceeding their previous best

---

[1] Robert Bly, *Iron John* (Reading, MA: Addison-Wesley Publishing Co., 1990), p.177.

performance. Being constantly pushed and challenged by their world-class rivals is a big part of what motivates them.

There is a curious camaraderie in sports competition. Top athletes want to duel a worthy opponent, one who will challenge them to achievements beyond their previous limits.

But it wouldn't have to be that way. In today's high tech world, for example, there is no need to travel to a common site at all. The decathlon competitors could just throw the javelin or run the hurdles at their home facility and electronic devices would broadcast the result to a common clearing house; after two days of virtual competition the scores could be totaled and a winner announced. They are, after all, ultimately competing against the clock and the tape measure.

Think of the reduced carbon footprint when no one has to leave home. In addition, it would give a new dimension to the derisive comment of an athlete "mailing in their game."

We propose that within a few months of this form of "competition," the athletes would be up in arms and would be refusing to participate in such a fiasco, such an abomination. This is not what the decathlon, or any other athletic event, is all about.

The Energy of Competition

There is an energy generated when human beings disagree with each other, when conflicts occur, when we compete; an energy that is not nearly as strong when everything is peaceful and quiet. Even in our most refined and enlightened moments, we gather into auditoriums to listen to students and intellectuals engage in public debates where spirited disagreement reigns. Behavioral scientists refer to this as "positive conflict" and regard it as a good thing.

We don't go to auditoriums to hear people agree with each other, unless they are all agreeing that some situation or policy needs to be changed, and we are offering them our support. We are energized and motivated and educated by honest and respectful disagreement, and this is one of the founding principles of our nation.

Competing With Disaster

An old, unattributed story, reputed to be true, takes place on the sea in pre-helicopter days. Back then, when a ship was disabled and being battered by winds and waves, the most important consideration was to get the crew off before the ship was lost. The only way to do this was to bring another ship close enough to the disabled vessel so that the men could be transferred, usually by ropes, from one vessel to the other.

It was sometimes too risky, in high seas, to bring the rescue ship close enough to the wallowing ship to allow the ropes to be deployed for the transfer; a sudden large swell might send the disabled ship crashing into the rescue ship and both crews would be lost.

The solution was to send a smaller boat, able to hold ten or fifteen men, to ferry the crew members back to the rescue vessel. This entailed a risk in itself, since the smaller boat would be less stable than the larger ships in the stormy seas. The success of the operation, and the lives of the crew, depended upon the skill and judgment of the man commanding the small boat.

The captain of the rescue ship chose his most trusted junior officer and gave him a choice: one of the smaller boats was powered by a gasoline engine, while the other depended upon a crew of oarsmen, rowing the boat across the treacherous waters between the two ships— certainly several times.

The officer, without hesitation, chose the boat propelled by the oarsmen.

(Continued)

(Continued)

The seas never relented, the wind was always fierce, but after hours of effort, all of the men had been rescued from the sinking ship. Needless to say, the oarsmen manning the small boat were completely exhausted, but they had been successful; everyone was safe.

The captain of the rescue ship, after ensuring that both crews had been cared for, approached his junior officer to offer his congratulations and thanks, and then asked:

"Why did you choose the boat with oars, and not the one with a motor?"

The officer answered quietly: "A motor can only do what it has been designed to do, never more. When you desperately need it, *a man can always reach inside and find strength to do more; to do what must be done.*"

The men in the boat were not competing with another team of oarsmen, but with the sea, with nature, with risk, with uncertainty. This is the difference between sport and life. This is why our use of the decathlon will always be a metaphor. You are not going for a gold medal; you are crafting your future.

You can reach success in the Decathlon Life by bringing out the best of who you are. You can generously work together with others, some of whom may appear to be competing with you, toward a common goal without focusing on who will be the winner and who will have to lose. The Decathlon Life is about exceeding your previous best, about reaching inside to find the resources, the strength, and the will to do what must be done—about ordinary people doing extraordinary things. It is an opportunity to rewrite the script; to write a new script for your future.

We celebrate your journey and your success.

CHAPTER 5

YOUR ADVISORY BOARD

Wow?

Bill was recently discussing this book with a very successful gentleman, one who is the founder and executive director of an influential and dynamic theatre that has redefined the regional theatre genre in greater Atlanta, a man who has received several personal awards for excellence and innovation in the creative, promotional and administrative policy areas of the dramatic arts. Bill was explaining his idea of suggesting that each Decathlon Life participant enroll and organize their own personal advisory board.

The gentleman looked shocked and said "An advisory board just for themselves? For their own projects? Individually?" Bill said "Yep."

The award winning executive chuckled and said, "Wow."

Bill still isn't sure if that was a "good wow" or a "bad wow."

Throughout this book you will find us referring to "...your advisory board." This is the place where we define what we mean by "advisory board" and tell you why we feel so strongly about them.

Defining the Advisory Board

The Decathlon Life, as we envision it, centers around you consciously crafting your unique future as opposed to reminiscing about your past.

If you are engaging in this journey, we suggest you recruit several people who will *advise* you as you go about accomplishing what you have committed to achieve. In the most basic sense, this is your advisory board.

There are not many other dimensions of the definition, but for the amusement of the lawyers reading the book, let's clear up some technical matters.

A lot of organizations have advisory boards—charities and libraries come to mind—and these differ from "Boards of Directors" in important ways:

- Advisory Boards have no formal or legal power; Boards of Directors do.

- A Board of Directors often can vote to remove an officer of the organization, an Advisory Board cannot.

- On the other hand, some Boards of Directors can be sued in court for improper or illegal behavior on the part of the organization; this is not true for a member of an Advisory Board.

- Finally, people serving on a Board of Directors usually are paid for their services; people serving on an Advisory Board usually are unpaid volunteers.

If your potential board candidate asks how much they are going to be paid, tell them you are protecting them from legal liability by paying them nada.

Benefits of Enrolling an Advisory Board

We don't suggest an advisory board on a whim; there are several benefits which will enhance your chances for achieving your Decathlon Life goals:

- Establishing the advisory board will provide you with a "sniff-test" for your commitment. If you cannot communicate your commitment with sufficient passion and clarity to enroll potential Advisory Board members, you need to rethink your goals and motivations. It is better to discover this during the ramp-up or start phase. There is nothing wrong or weak about redefining or changing your commitment; in fact, it shows that you are engaged in discovering and choosing what you can passionately be committed to achieve.

- When you successfully enroll your board, you will have established a new array of eyes and ears to help you evaluate the landscape ahead. We guarantee they will not see things exactly as you do, and if you ask what they are seeing and hearing and listen well to their observations, they will be of exceptional value to you. See how a diverse collection of committed observers and a more innovative view of the future can change everything in the chapters on the Discus and the High Jump.

- In the same way, the personal strengths, experience, and wisdom that the Board members bring will be different from yours. Not better or worse, just different. They have knowledge you do not have, insights you will not come up with, intuition that is theirs alone; if you have enrolled them, they want to share this with you. All of their life experiences, their hard-won wisdom, when shared and paired with yours, will increase your odds of success. More on this in the chapters on the Shot Put and the 110 Meter Hurdles.

- You are not only expanding and strengthening your own network of friends and associates; you are potentially gaining access to the professional and personal networks of your board members. If one of them offers "I know a lady on the City Council; let me call her and ask her about meeting with you," you have potentially saved an enormous amount of time and effort. A board member may even suggest having one of their friends visit the board to hear the discussion and offer suggestions. See the chapter on the Javelin and leverage. It just keeps getting better for your project.

- You will discover that your board members can help you focus, clarify, and expand your vision – that picture of the future that you are committed to create. They will not be trying to do this, or even know that it is occurring, but you will see it happening and be amazed. They are helping you expand your boundaries and clarify your perspective. See the Long Jump and Pole Vault chapters.

- You may—this does not always happen—see the beginning of the formation of a *team*. There are lots of definitions of a "team," but you will know it if one shows up. We are ultimately motivated by a desire to achieve fulfillment (See the blocked area below for more on how this works). If you are fortunate enough to create a team, you have been blessed. This can be a life-changing journey for all of you, truth be told.

- Chances are good that one of your Advisory Board members will, through their experience of serving with you, be motivated to launch their own Decathlon Life adventure. If they do, chances are good that they will enroll you for their Advisory Board. The script and the stage set will change, and your role will be different, but just think: you can do it all again!

- When all is said and done, you've got folks who will help you organize a celebration! They, along with others who joined along the way, are your celebrities. You will find more information on celebrities in the chapter on the 1500 Meters.

Personal Fulfillment and Team Fulfillment

People are motivated by doing things that fulfill them, that fulfill who they are, and we are ultimately fulfilled by doing what we do best. We all have unique talents and skills and when we use them in what we do every day, we do our work well and we are fulfilled.

But this is *personal* fulfillment, and there is also a phenomenon called *team* fulfillment.

Consider the example of the marching band. High school and college marching bands spend an enormous amount of time learning to execute elaborate drills and formations while playing music; the best bands travel to regional and national contests to compete against each other and, if they are chosen as the best of the best, they are invited to march in parades sponsored by Macy's or the Rose Bowl.

Individual band members must be good at playing their instruments. They audition as trombone players or drummers to be selected to be in the band. Then long hours of practice begin so that they can play their music at a professional level while marching across an athletic field to spell out a cursive "Ohio." Thank goodness it isn't "Pennsylvania."

(Continued)

The individual marching band member must be a talented trombone or saxophone or whatever player to be selected for the band and this member must spend time on their own honing their talent as a trombone player and learning their part in all of the musical selections the band plays (there may be dozens).

But then the hard work begins.

The band members learn circle drills and other complex choreographies. They also learn leadership and discipline; there is no "follow the leader" in marching band; if you want to compete with the big kids, every member must move through incredibly difficult routines with perfect timing and footwork. While playing a musical instrument. And playing a repertoire of a half dozen musical selections. *Perfectly.*

But here's the kicker: there are no individual awards in these competitions; there is no "National Best Trombone Player." The band competes as the entire band; sixty or eighty or one hundred students, aged fourteen to twenty-three, compete strictly as a unit. The atmosphere is electric, the competition is intense and the students are incredibly motivated.

They are motivated by *team fulfillment*.

In competitive sports there are team championships but there are also individual player's statistics and all-star teams. We are satisfying both team and personal fulfillment. For marching bands, it is team fulfillment only.

This does not seem to dampen down the passion and intensity and commitment displayed by the students participating in the marching band.

It almost seems to magnify them.

Team fulfillment is a powerful motivator. When we say "You will know when a team shows up," this is what we mean.

Our wish is that all of you discover you have created a motivated team.

Rules for the Advisory Board

There are no rules. Make up your own. Better yet, let your board make up their own.

Picking the Board

Usually, as a rule, we don't make rules, so let's refer to these as two very strong recommendations regarding who you include on your advisory board.

First, we recommend that you enroll at least one member under the age of twenty-five. Our society is changing and the pace of change is increasing. All of us in the Boomer generation need some help dealing with social networks like Facebook and Twitter, where most of the communications flow will occur in the future. While we could spend our time climbing up a very steep learning curve, it seems to us to make more sense to let our newer generation members guide us through our inadequacies.

Two Sides of the Room

Much has been written about the different ways the several generations communicate with each other. There was a recent seminar at Kennesaw State University where business executives and college professors were on one side of the room, and college students were on the other. The speaker pointed out that most of the participants on the "professor" side of the room would use email or the telephone to correspond with the world and each other, while the "student" side would use texting or social networks. In addition, in three years time the professors will still be emailing or phoning, while the students will have discarded texting and/or existing networks and gone on to something entirely new.

(Continued)

(Continued)

Most of us in the Boomer generation spent the majority of our careers communicating with people by telephone, snail mail, or face to face; our written communications were usually formal confirmation of what we had already agreed upon informally.

Today, the preponderance of corporate business communication is conducted via email, posts to internal networks and occasional video or audio conferences. A Fortune 500 executive with international responsibilities recently told us that she had people on her staff that she had never met face-to-face.

As a Decathlon Life practitioner, you may want to leave all that behind, and handle all of your communications in the dinosaur mode, and you have every right to make that decision. You are your own boss, after all.

On the other hand, if you intend to have your voice heard, and contribute your wisdom and experience to the world, we suggest you take some time to develop or enroll some competence in electronic communications and social networking. Note that we included the option of *enrolling* this competence; bringing someone onto your Advisory Board who has experience and skills in developing websites and utilizing social networks is well worth your consideration. As one Boomer pointed out, in a pinch you could always enlist some help from your grandchildren.

We also believe that the members of the younger generation, the "star children" (as they have been defined) have more to teach us than just technical skills. Much of what they have to contribute we have not yet discovered or defined. We encourage you to be open to discovering more of what they are to teach us and to report back to us other Boomers so that we can begin to give them and their talents and their wisdom the respect and attention they deserve.

Finally, we believe that we have something to contribute to the younger generations, and that this is best done at short range. Bill explains more in a story:

Crafting Your Future, Take Two

I was attending a seminar in Orlando recently and from the audience I mentioned The Decathlon Life book and our concept of crafting your future. During a break, I talked with a young man, perhaps in his mid-twenties, and the conversation turned to the advisory boards.

I explained why I think people engaged in the Decathlon Life in their sixties or seventies should try to enroll people from the young man's generation, in their twenties, for their advisory boards. I said that I feel younger people bring a different energy, a better appreciation of a big portion of the culture, and a propensity for innovation and technology. The Boomer generation, I said, needs that.

In return, I continued, the older members of the advisory board could offer the younger members their years of experience, perhaps a different approach on people skills, and a longer range perspective on current events and trends. I think both generations have something to contribute and something to learn from each other and that serving together on advisory boards offers a creative way to accomplish that.

The young man's reply stunned me. "I agree," he said. "What struck me, as you were talking about your book, is that the challenge you are offering your readers—'How are you going to craft your future?'—is the same challenge people my age are dealing with every day. We would love to know how people have dealt with this question over a lifetime and what worked for them and what didn't. I can see that being on a Decathlon Life advisory board could be a terrific opportunity."

The second of our two recommendations is that you consider enrolling your most unlikely choice for your advisory board.

Having Your Most Unlikely Choice on Your Advisory Board

This is the person who bugs you the most, who you disagree with most often, who is just an argument looking for a place to happen.

But did it ever occur to you that you manage somehow to keep this person in your life? There are lots of other people you disagree with who you just avoid or ignore, but this particular one seems to hang around just to irritate you. They are so different, so much a polar opposite to you that they drive you batty. Why in the world would we suggest that you ask for their opinions, their advice?

Well, it just might be because you married them.

"Opposites Attract"

You've no doubt heard this before. Psychologists like Dr. Phil tell us it's absolutely true. This is human nature's little obstacle course, pairing you with someone who pushes all your buttons.

In the great scheme of things, according to the experts, this is how we grow, how we keep from being polarized, how we extend our boundaries. We pick someone who looks perfectly normal but in fact has been put on this earth to keep us from being too full of ourselves, to challenge us to occasionally get beyond the end of our nose.

If the person we are describing here is the *last* person that you would want on your advisory board, it is virtually essential that you enroll them. This might be a good time to bring them up to date on what you have planned for the rest of your life.

Disagreement generates energy, clarity, and a chance to engage in honest analysis. Absorbing and including disagreement while sustaining the relationship generates wisdom; painful as it is, it calls forth the best of who you want to be.

Besides, wonder of wonders, you might both find that you and your most unlikely choice actually enjoy working together, at least some of the time. Now isn't that worth the pain?

Taking the Big Step

So why mess up your burgeoning Decathlon Life by including a potential terrorist on your board? We propose that there are several reasons you might consider:

- When two people in a committed relationship work together to accomplish something bigger than either of them, and in fact bigger than their relationship, it can totally transform their respect for and compassion for each other. This is the universe's short-form marriage seminar.

- If you get involved in your Decathlon Life and you realize you are going to live longer than you thought, don't you want to bring them along too? Who else would do such a good job of keeping you humble?

- Your differing perspectives will ensure that your project will be evaluated and analyzed from two totally contrasting positions and this more intense scrutiny will give you a much better shot at achieving success. After all, you are engaged in crafting your future, and success in this endeavor can be fairly significant.

- If you can't enroll the person who knows you best to be on your team, you probably aren't ready to enroll anyone else. Think through your project and your motives again and ask yourself if you are being honest with yourself. Our culture rewards inauthentic behavior at every turn; if we are not careful we will become immune to the danger and become inauthentic with ourselves. This is your opportunity to find out what is *really* important to you and *why*. When you answer those questions honestly and truthfully, people will want to be on your team, to enroll in your cause.

THE DISCUS

CHAPTER 6

THE DISCUS

Committed Beginner

You're in the Game

So you have chosen your commitment and have developed a plan to get started. You may even be well on your way. Congratulations! You are in the game!

You may have chosen something new, or something you have always enjoyed doing but haven't had time to fully develop, or just something that needs to be done.

In some cases you may be entering the realm of Committed Beginner.

Let's talk about the Discus!

The discus throw was one of the events of the original ancient Greek pentathlon. One of the iconic treasures of early Grecian art is a statue of a discus thrower, crouching and ready to uncoil and release the heavy disk.

Before it was a sport, the discus throw was a battlefield weapon system, with skilled throwers hurling the lethal stone or metal disk at a high rate of speed into the enemy lines. The spinning disk was the pre-explosive equivalent of a high velocity cannon ball. Even today, with throwers wielding disks weighing almost five pounds, if you participate in a modern track and field event you learn to keep your eyes open for errant disks or javelins.

The modern throwing technique may not have significantly changed in the last 2,500 years or so. The throw is made from inside a ring about eight feet in diameter. The thrower begins by crouching with his back to the path of the throw. He winds up by twisting further away from the launch path, spinning one and a half times counterclockwise across the ring to build momentum. He launches the disk at an angle so that it will ride the air currents aerodynamically. It is a beautiful sport to watch; a well thrown discus can soar for more than 170 feet, over half the length of a football field.

But throwing the discus is not an easy sport to master. There is something counterintuitive about the discus throw.

You would think, as the competitor spins counterclockwise around the ring, building up centrifugal momentum to maximize the energy of the launch—you would think that you would release the disk off the *little finger* of the throwing hand, with the disk spinning counterclockwise, the same direction as the competitor's momentum.

You would be wrong.

Let's take a look at the physics of throwing a discus.

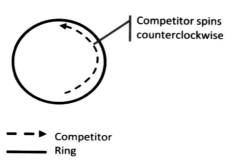

Competitor spins counterclockwise

- - ▶ Competitor
——— Ring

For a right handed thrower (all of these examples assume a right handed thrower), the discus is released off the *index finger* in such a way that it spins *clockwise*, opposite the spin of the competitor.

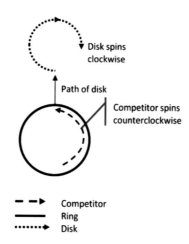

Disk spins clockwise

Path of disk

Competitor spins counterclockwise

- - ▶ Competitor
——— Ring
•••••▶ Disk

Spinning the disk clockwise balances the counterclockwise momentum of the thrower and allows the disk to travel in a straight path. The aerodynamic lift provided by the balanced rotational momentum results in dramatically longer throws. It is not an easy technique to master, but mastery is necessary if you intend to be a competitor in the discus throw.

For the person mastering the Decathlon Life, there is a lesson here, perhaps even a warning: things are not always as they seem, or as the general consensus opinion assumes them to be.

Bill's Engineering Degree

From Bill:

I was thirty when I left Procter and Gamble and the manufacturing world and began training to sell mainframe computers for IBM. This was in the mid 1960s; only the largest companies had computers and many of them had only automated two or three business functions. I had never sold anything in my life, my second child had just been born, I was moving my family from Chicago to Atlanta, and I had only seen one computer in my life. It was all very exciting, but also occasionally nerve-wracking.

I was hired into IBM by the Branch Manager of the Atlanta Manufacturing Branch Office; our office represented IBM to manufacturing organizations in Atlanta and central Georgia. With my engineering degree and manufacturing background, it was a good fit for me. I was a rookie, but an experienced rookie.

One day early in my training, my Branch Manager said that he understood why I was motivated to begin a new career in sales but wanted to know why I chose to come to IBM and sell computers rather than staying with P&G and selling their products.

I said that with my engineering degree and MBA, I thought I could better explain the highly technical computers to the executives of the manufacturing companies that made up my soon-to-be sales territory, leaving unsaid my opinion that said executives would recognize how smart I was and how well prepared I was to help lead their company into a glorious and highly technical future. I went on at length about how important a resource I would be to my customers and prospects.

My manager listened patiently and then said "I'm going to tell you something you will never forget." He was right about that, of course; this retelling is proof of that.

(Continued)

(Continued)

He leaned back and said "People buy things from people they like."

I waited. He went on.

"If you buy a suit of clothes, or an ice cream cone, or an automobile, or a computer from someone, and you like the person who sold it to you, and you like the experience and the way you were treated, you will go back to that person again, and you will recommend them to your friends, and now and then you may even try to find ways to make them successful."

What he said had nothing to do with my engineering degree, but I immediately knew that he was right. No, more than right, what he said was *profound*, and had application far beyond my career, beyond just selling things to people.

At that moment I became a *committed beginner* in the sales arena and every day I found his words to be pure gold. In fact, what he said changed the way I lived my life.

I began to shift my attention from proving how smart and valuable I was to spending time finding out what my customers needed to become more successful in their marketplaces. I found that people appreciate it when you work hard at helping them succeed.

If you are choosing a commitment that leads you into a new arena, I recommend exploring the role of committed beginner.

The Committed Beginner

The committed beginner is a very powerful concept, one that can, like the flight of the discus, give you leverage and lift, can cause you to soar, to craft a rest-of-your-life that is a thing of beauty. Let's look at the construction of the term:

- *Commitment* is, of course all-important. It is what gets you out of bed in the morning. Commitment provides a strong measure of determination, of resourcefulness, of energy, of persistence, of intention to exceed your previous best. We all know what commitment involves; it is the foundation, the platform for establishing and living a Decathlon Life.

- The concept of being the *beginner*, however, is not so well known. It is the spirit of being the beginner that makes us more open, curious, searching; willing to discover what we don't know. We become passionate about learning, hungry to form productive and mutually supportive relationships with others, some of whom are beginners like us, some of whom are seasoned veterans in the arena into which we have ventured.

You can begin to see that the combination of determination and curiosity, of intention and openness, of the passion of commitment and the spirit of the beginner can be a powerful resource.

Denmark: Living Your Life Purpose

A small consulting firm in Copenhagen, Denmark, established by Flemming Christensen and Claus Roager Olsen, is earning an international reputation for their prowess in teaching businesses how to create and manage effective project teams. Their firm achieves breakthrough results by enabling people in an organization to work more effectively together to achieve personal and organizational goals.

Bill attended a seminar that Flemming delivers to executives in an organization; Flemming's intention is to help the executives understand and live their life purpose. It could as well illustrate the way to tap into the commitment of the Decathlon Life and discovering the spirit of the beginner. Early in his seminars Flemming projected on the screen a picture of a five-year-old child looking away from the camera, down a long, empty rural road. Flemming asked the seminar participants to recall: "What were you like when you were five?"

(Continued)

(Continued)

He began recording their responses on a white board:

Trusting. Optimistic. Creative. Curious. Absorbed. Engaged. Energetic. Innovative.

Flemming told the executives that when they discovered their life purpose and begin to live into that purpose they would start to recover these characteristics from childhood; they would find a new wind at their backs. Their lives will take on a new luster; they would regain the zest for living that they once experienced. He has the evidence, from other executives and other seminars over the years, to support what he told them. He proved to be right.

The Spirit of the Beginner

We propose that the characteristics identified by Flemming's seminar participants are also the characteristics of the committed beginner. Life can become more fulfilling as we choose to be beginners, and as we pursue committed accomplishments in arenas that are both familiar and new in our Decathlon Life.

The Ever-Present Advisory Board

This is an excellent place to call upon your Advisory Board. Do they have expertise in some aspect of your new endeavor? Can they coach you, or do they know someone who can? Your Board is usually the best place to begin your search for what works.

Remember that the decathlon is not a team sport; in the arena you are competing on your own. Preparing for the competition, however, and learning to become a better competitor definitely do require teamwork, and the beginner's spirit will serve you well.

One to a Customer

Out of the mouths of babes (and committed beginners): Betty talks about one of her sons:

My boys were coin collectors when they were very young and I remember that one day they were hiding under their covers, Michael and David. I grabbed one, trying to figure out which was which, and Michael popped up and announced "I'm Michael Siegel, in mint condition. Only one to a customer."

And he got it. Absolutely got it. We are all "one to a customer." There is only one Michael Siegel, nee these thirty-plus years later; there is only one David Siegel, one Betty Siegel, and one Joel Siegel. We all started as beginners and we can recapture the innocence, the openness, the "mint condition" whenever we choose.

The Discus

The lesson of the discus: things are not always as they seem. As you craft your Decathlon Life, distinguish between the areas of expertise where you are the wise mentor and areas where you are the committed beginner. You will probably have opportunities to play both roles, and we wish you great joy in playing both of them.

THE LONG JUMP

CHAPTER 7

THE LONG JUMP

Expanding Boundaries

Proceed With Caution? Not!

Things may be opening up for you now, with opportunities and challenges both coming into view.

Sometimes all of the newness and change can be unsettling, even intimidating; sometimes you may feel that you are exceeding your comfort level.

Is it time to slow down, to move more carefully, more cautiously?

Welcome to the realm of the Long Jump!

The long jump is about expanding your boundaries.

We all have a comfort zone—in fact, many of them. We will talk about this subject with our children or our friends, but not about that. We will take on *this* volunteer effort, become a member of *this* group, stand for *this* principle, speak up about *this* policy, but not that one, not those, not them.

These are some of our boundaries.

These boundaries come from a lifetime of being practical; of choosing what can be done versus what might be done, learning what works and deciding what we should settle for. As children, our boundaries keep us safe and secure; as adults, they keep us from failing, being disappointed, or being embarrassed. It is part of wisdom, say we. It is a mark of maturity to know how far we can go, how much we can push. We have honed our ability to apply good judgment all of our lives and we are known for being paragons of circumspection. They are our boundaries; we have chosen them carefully and defended them well. They help define who we are. Why would we question them?

The long jump is about bringing our boundaries up for observation and evaluation.

The Ancient Long Jump

As one of the original events of the Olympic Games of ancient Greece, you would expect the long jump to be a battlefield maneuver, and you would be right. The fighting of that period was mainly hand-to-hand, and the terrain of the battlefield played a big part in the outcome—hills, streams, ravines, forests and other natural features could be used to a warrior's advantage if he were skilled and kept his head about him.

The ability to jump across a small stream or ravine, or to bypass a damaged footbridge, would, in effect, *expand the boundaries of the battlefield* for a warrior who might otherwise be trapped by an enemy force. By including the long jump in the original Olympics, the Greeks demonstrated the value they placed in developing this martial skill. The warriors with great leaping ability were more likely to survive to compete against their enemies on the playing field, as well as the battlefield. By expanding the amount of the terrain that was accessible to them, they created many more options and possibilities than were available just a moment before.

Expanding our boundaries can be like that. In ancient days, expanding our boundaries prolonged life; in modern times, expanding our boundaries can enrich and fulfill our lives.

The Modern Long Jump

Long jumping is relatively uncomplicated. We probably learned the essentials before we were five years old; you run as fast as you can to build momentum and then see how far you can jump. In competition, the long jumper runs down a pathway, builds speed and momentum, plants his or her foot on a board built into the pathway and launches into the air. The jumper attempts to thrust their body both forward and upward; the higher the competitor can soar in the arc of their jump, the longer they will stay in the air and the further their momentum will carry them. The jumper lands in a sand-filled pit. The jump is measured from the edge of the take-off board to the mark in the sand made by the landing. World class long jumpers can reach distances approaching or exceeding twenty-nine feet.

Not a particularly glamorous sport, but one that comes with a wealth of metaphorical insight.

Crafting Our Future

In our retirement years, our "golden years," there can be a subtle withdrawal from the world, a kind of retreat from the rat race. The La-Z-Boy sings its siren song: take two beers and call me in the morning.

The Decathlon Life, based on consciously crafting your future, has many different dimensions and possibilities, but almost all of them will include getting off the couch.

The subset of Boomer retirees that we call "engaged" will run up against their boundaries on a regular basis, sometimes without recognizing them as boundaries. As we pointed out at the beginning of this chapter, boundaries often just appear as ways of being practical, of not being radical, of going along to get along.

Sometimes "radical" behavior can make all the difference:

George Washington Expands His Boundaries

In December of 1776, George Washington was losing the War for American Independence. The British had captured and occupied New York and had chased Washington's small army across New Jersey and into Pennsylvania. Morale was low, the Colonials were facing a vastly superior force, and Washington was in danger of having his men lose heart and just walk away and go home. He was perhaps down to his last chance.

On December 19, 1776, Thomas Paine published the pamphlet *The American Crisis* ("These are the times that try men's souls…"). Washington had it read to his men.

General Washington was preparing to expand his boundaries.

On Christmas night, 1776, Washington crossed the Delaware River with a hastily assembled invasion force of about 2,000 troops and surprised the British garrison at Trenton. The Hessian soldiers encamped there thought that the Delaware River was one of the boundaries of the battlefield; Washington chose to challenge that.

The Colonials captured 1,000 enemy soldiers and some badly needed supplies and sent an unmistakable message to the British: we aren't even thinking about giving up. George Washington, with one bold move, had created a whole new set of possibilities.

He ultimately did the job he was chosen to do: he commanded the troops that won the war. He continued to expand his boundaries however; he was elected the first President of the United States and he has become known as "the Indispensible Man" and "The Father of Our Country." Boundaries? What boundaries?

Not for Everyone

Expanding our boundaries requires some degree of self-inspection, even if it is a seemingly instantaneous thing. People react differently to expanding boundaries because people are different. None of us see the world exactly like someone else does. This does not make us good or bad, better or worse; just different. People who choose to keep the boundaries they have are not wrong; theirs is the only life they have and they have a right to live it as they choose.

For those thousands of engaged individuals entering the ranks of the retired every day, however, the choice may be a more aggressive one. Not all of them will have a George Washington moment, but a high percentage of them will have the opportunity to go beyond their comfort zone, to expand their boundaries, in various ways, big and small. The long jump is a metaphor for seizing these opportunities more often than not, and becoming increasingly willing to take on risks and challenges as our boundaries expand—and they will expand. Betty tells about expanding her career boundaries:

Betty Expands Her Boundaries

After a memorable start, I had settled into a career as a Dean at the University of Florida. What made it memorable was the way in which, over time, the other Deans (all men) began to accept me as a woman and not as a woman who could think like a man. Introducing a woman into what had always been a no-girls-allowed club was a courageous thing to do in that day. The Deans of the University met regularly to discuss policy and procedures, and suddenly there I was in their midst; pleasant, friendly, but no shrinking violet. They soon began to respect my judgment and the subtle ways I could poke their traditions in the ribs.

(Continued)

(Continued)

I had already made my impression as the first female professor in one of the most important departments on campus, particularly when I arrived on campus very pregnant with my second child. The Dean said that they planned for me to start teaching right away and weren't prepared to cover a long maternity leave but I told them I planned to have the baby during the semester break and be ready to go when classes resumed. Of course that's exactly what happened. I delivered on the Friday night that exams were over, graded the exams on Saturday and Sunday while feeding the baby; my husband Joel walked the grades to the University on Monday. From that day forward they referred to me as "that woman" when they needed something, as in "Get that woman as the speaker."

Several years later, one of my friends was in my office talking about having spent the weekend visiting a small school in Georgia, about 4,000 students, close to Atlanta. My friend talked about how friendly, vital, and energetic the campus atmosphere seemed. The name of the school was Kennesaw College.

I remembered the name but couldn't remember why. Rummaging through the mail on my desk, I found a letter from Kennesaw College. It was an inquiry letter; the college was searching for a new President and was inviting me to apply. The deadline was that day. I called the college and asked for and received an extension. That started the most unexpected string of events.

I retired in 2006 after twenty-five years as the President of Kennesaw State University, which now has an enrollment of over 24,000 students.

Expanding our boundaries usually involves going beyond our comfort zones, and that raises issues of rationality and risk. Up until now, preserving our comfort zone seemed like the rational thing to do, and now we are casting caution to the winds. Not everyone can relate to that, unless circumstances demand it.

The choice may be dictated by exceptional circumstances—that was certainly the case in Washington's choice to cross the Delaware—and it very likely would have been the case in ancient Greece when a warrior was being chased by a group of angry enemies.

One of Bill's favorite stories about responding to exceptional circumstances comes from time he spent in Colorado:

A Hunter Expands His Boundaries

The story goes, that two hunters in the west were talking about grizzly bears and the danger they represented. One man remarked that he had once been chased by a grizzly.

"Yeah I was! I was in a meadow, in a little valley upside of a mountain, and across the meadow I saw a grizzly just as he saw me! I didn't have my gun or nuthin'. I started hightailin' it toward some trees, but the grizzly was gainin' on me and I knew I was in trouble. Just then I saw an old dead tree, closer to me than the other trees, and I started headin' for that.

As I got closer, and the bear was gettin' closer too, breathin' down my neck, I saw the tree only had one limb and it was fifteen or twenty feet off the ground. It was my only chance, to jump up and grab that limb."

"Are you telling me you jumped up twenty feet off the ground and grabbed a limb on a tree?"

"I missed it on the way up but I got it on the way back down."

You may be on the advisory board of someone who jumps up and grabs the limb. Consider yourself blessed, and tell them that you knew all along that they had it in them. Because they do. We all do.

You may be the one who grabs the limb. If you successfully expand your boundaries, you will have a story to tell to others, and an opportunity to set something profound in motion. There are many in our world who are looking for normal people, people like themselves, who have grabbed the limb. They just want to know that it can be done.

Whatever the circumstances, the long jump reminds us that we have the power to go beyond our comfort zones, to do things we never knew we could or should do, and the choice, as always, is ours. Expanding your boundaries is an exceptionally powerful tool to use in crafting your future.

Post Script

Expanding boundaries is not always sweetness and light. You may find yourself in some difficulty, and the whole thing suddenly seems like a bad idea. You never knew something could be so tough, so frustrating; no wonder nobody has ever done this particular thing before. Besides, you're too old to be doing this kind of thing anyway.

That's when it is time to huddle with your advisory board. Sit down with at least two members and lay it all out; what you intended to accomplish, what worked, what didn't work, what the situation is right now and just how you feel about it all. Let them hash it all out; you be the witness on the stand and answer their questions as accurately as you can. Open up your frustration and fear of failure for all to see.

If your board says for you to back off and either re-design your project or choose a new one, follow their advice. It will make you and your group into a *team*.

If they say to jump for the branch, put your jumping shoes on. Expanding your boundaries can be exhilarating, and now you have partners committed to your success.

THE SHOT PUT

CHAPTER 8

THE SHOT PUT

Personal Strengths

Crafting Your Future

The word "craft" is derived from the Old High German word *kraft* which translates as "strength." For thousands of years, craftsmen have used their talents, their skills, their *strengths* to contribute who they are and what they bring to their world.

What are your personal strengths? What will you use to craft your Decathlon Life?

Welcome to the world of the Shot Put!

The shot put is the decathlon event which requires the greatest pure physical strength. Champion shot putters are big, strong and agile, with the emphasis on strong.

As you craft your Decathlon Life, the shot put serves as a reminder to consolidate your own personal strengths, your lifetime of experience, and your accumulated and hard-earned wisdom. These are three different resources and those differences need to be dealt with, but first let's look at the shot put event.

The Modern Shot Put

"Putting" the "shot" is really pushing or launching a sixteen pound metal ball from within a seven-foot-wide "ring" without stepping outside the ring.

Legend says that Greek warriors competed in throwing heavy stones during the siege of Troy, and medieval soldiers reputedly measured how far they could throw a cannonball. We do know that the first Modern Olympic Games (1896) included the shot put event.

Putting the shot is an exceptionally straightforward event; there is little subtlety involved. The rules state that the shot must be held and released at shoulder level or above. Power and distance comes from the movement across the ring and the athlete's strength. The only difference in technique among competitors is how they move their feet and legs. Original shot putters faced away from the direction of the launch and used a "glide" step across the ring; most competitors today swing their forward leg to generate rotational momentum as they move into the put.

The key, as it has always been, is physical strength, but it is vitally important for the competitor to harness their strength and to direct it toward the goal. The men's world distance record for the sixteen pound shot is over seventy-five feet, a prodigious accomplishment.

Why do we care about this rather simple, uncomplicated event? What is the value of the shot put as a metaphor for crafting your future?

Identifying and Directing Your Personal Strengths

Few of us in our sixties and beyond are possessed of exceptional physical strength, but all of us have personal strengths, those unique talents and skills which help to define us and identify our individual contribution to those around us, our community, and our larger society. We may be very familiar with these strengths, or they may be relatively unknown to us.

Personal Strengths

Bill has spent the last ten years researching, writing about and speaking about a topic variously referred to as personality models, personal strengths or a number of other descriptive terms. You may know some of the personality models by their more popular names such as Myers-Briggs (or MBTI), DiSC, the Enneagram, True Colors, Strengths Finder and more.

Some people swear by these tools, others swear at them. Many people have taken tests to identify their "type," only to find that the tests are often not reproducible; that is, you can take a test several times and receive different scores.

What we do know is that people are different, and there are models which try to organize and explain those differences so that we can find what it is that we do best, what our strengths or talents are. These models have been around for thousands of years (i.e. the signs of Astrology) and have been in use across many cultures (i.e. the Chinese Zodiac). There is evidence that portions of Homer's Odyssey were written as a teaching tool for a personality model.

You may want to explore these tools on your own, in order to help you discover what your strengths are, what you do best. Our web site, www.thedecathlonlife.com contains links to several other sites where you can learn more about the models and, in some cases, take a test to help determine your "type."

In crafting your unique future, you will have an enormous leg up when you can identify and focus your personal strengths. If you are playing to your strengths, if you are doing what you do best, you are continuously becoming more of who you are. The personal fulfillment you experience from doing what you do best and becoming more of who you are will motivate you and keep you in the game.

Be yourself. Everyone else is taken.
                                                                —Oscar Wilde

---

Bill relates some surprising experiences around personality models:

I Don't Think I Want to Know

In leading seminars on personality models, I would introduce the various "types" that made up the model and offer clues on how to recognize them from people's everyday behavior. On the first cycle through the model, everybody could recognize somebody—their spouse, their boss, their father, etc. A few could recognize themselves. The next step was to have the participants turn to a neighbor and take turns discussing the clues in their own behavior that would allow them to discover their probable type. It's always easier to see the other person's type than it is to see yours.

After a few minutes of paired sharing, almost everybody had picked their type; this was "who they were." In many cases, identifying their type was expressed with a feeling of relief: "I'm not crazy, I'm just an INTJ!" The room was alive with the energy of discovery.

Then, as part of the seminar, I started describing the kinds of careers that each type might feel comfortable in. All of these participants were from business organizations, many from Fortune 500 companies. Many were a decade or two into their careers.

(Continued)

(Continued)

Most of them were in a career that had no relation to their personality type.

The atmosphere in the room went from elation to gloom to determined resignation in a matter of minutes. "Never mind about my career, how can I better manage my people now that I can understand how they see things? It's good that now I know more about them."

In that vein (and I was prepared for it) the seminar continued.

It is not our intention to reform the way corporations develop their employees' career paths, even though the Gallup Company found that only about one out of every four employees in the typical organization is "doing what they do best."[2]

Rather, we relate this to you to give you a heads-up: if you spent your career in a large organization, there is a 75% chance that what you did for a living is not what you do best. In other words, don't assume that because you were an accountant for forty-five years, accounting is your personal strength. You have an exceptional career experience as an accountant and that is of great value, but your strength may be in getting contentious people to work together.

The key—in life as well as in the shot put—is identifying your strengths, focusing them and using them in such a way that they enable you to achieve your committed goal. In crafting your Decathlon Life, we encourage you to go a step further and consolidate your strengths with your experience and wisdom.

---

[2] Marcus Buckingham and Curt Coffman, *First, Break All the Rules* (New York: Simon and Schuster, 1999).

Consolidating Your Experience

Just as we all have personal strengths to draw upon, we also have unique experiences that we can use to craft our Decathlon Life.

Most people reading this book have decades of experience dealing with hundreds or thousands of situations, people, challenges, opportunities realized and missed, decisions good and not so good. It all adds up to an exceptional resource to be drawn upon; there is really no substitute for experience, and your bank account is full and ready to be tapped. The best part is, no matter how much you draw upon your experience account, the balance just keeps getting larger.

This is an enormous resource for you, your team, and your community. This is one time that focusing on the past and not the future can be vital for crafting your Decathlon Life. What have you experienced that can make your future more fulfilling? Where can your experience be of value to you in achieving your committed goal? Where can it be of value to your larger community? How will you combine it with your personal strengths?

Consolidating Your Wisdom

Wisdom is defined in some dictionaries as being comprised of knowledge, insight and judgment. These are qualities that tend to be improved and sharpened over time; we would expect them to be more present and more fully developed in people of retirement age. Why would we want to suddenly discount the value or ignore the contribution of people who have retired from an everyday job but who still intend to have an impact on their world?

Experience can have many dimensions and be applicable in many domains, and a person may have experience in a particular field (healthcare, for example, or academics or real estate or marketing; the list is endless) or in broader categories such as choosing the right person for a challenging job, or building and leading a team.

Wisdom is more general, more applicable to all domains, even to fields in which the person has no experience, but it is not as readily explained or demonstrated. Saying "I spent forty-five years in hospitals and clinics" is very different from saying "I am a good judge of people." One can be substantiated with evidence; the other depends upon the perception of the observer.

The qualities of insight and judgment as enumerated in the dictionary definition of wisdom above are associated with the Gut as opposed to the Mind in the Greek model of human consciousness (Mind, Heart, and Gut). This suggests that developing your intuitive (Gut) talents could result in a perceived increase in wisdom. There is additional information about the Greek consciousness model, including distinguishing between instinct and intuition, in Chapter 9 and the 110 Meter Hurdles.

Building Your Support Team

When you look at the composition of your advisory board, knowing what your strengths are and being able to recognize the strengths of others gives you the ability to build your team in a more inclusive and creative manner. Betty commented on this a while back in a speech she gave in her best demure, Southern-belle manner:

> If you have a team on which you have all men, you've got trouble! If you have all women, you've got trouble! I mean trouble in the sense that you're not touching all the bases. It takes a quadrant to be successful.
>
> I'm an Expressive, a driving expressive, and I want it done yesterday. I need a Driver on my team; I need an Amiable on my team; I need an Analytical on my team. That's what we are saying.
>
> (Continued)

(Continued)

Actually, we're talking about honoring diversity. That is what women have brought to the table. We have opened up whole new doors in which we look at people in a different way and honor diversity.

If I come back from a meeting and say I have this wonderful idea, my driver vice presidents say "Here we go again, there's no way we can do it; we don't have the money." What do you think my analytical says? "We'll study it; we'll give it a look." For days the printouts will rise higher and higher. What does my amiable say? He says, "We can sell it; pour some coffee!"

If we were all expressives what would happen? We would kill each other! We'd churn out hundreds of ideas and then throw them all out. If we have all drivers we'll kill each other because each of us believes we are absolutely the best thinker on campus. What's wrong with all analyticals? We'll study it to death! What about all amiables? We'll all grow fat together!

We all have a piece of the puzzle, and each piece is unique. The shot put reminds us that our piece is exceptionally valuable and unique because no one else has it. Our personal strengths are our vehicle for contributing who we are to our world. When these strengths are consolidated with our lifetime experience and our accumulated wisdom we have resources that we can uniquely bring to bear in the future we are crafting. Don't let your piece of the puzzle go missing.

THE 110 METER HURDLES

CHAPTER 9

THE 110 METER HURDLES

Instinct and Intuition

Developing All of Your Resources

Lurking below the surface of the talents, experience and strengths we use every day are two other very valuable resources: instinct and intuition.

The ancient Greeks thought human beings could develop and improve our personal capabilities in three distinct areas: Mental (dealing with the mind), Emotional (dealing with the heart) and Instinctive (dealing with the gut).

We don't pay much attention to our instinctive capabilities these days.

And have you ever watched someone run the hurdles?

Yogi Berra, New York Yankees baseball legend, once said "You can't think and hit at the same time."

The same is true for competitive hurdling. The 110 meter hurdles race is over in less than fifteen seconds, during which time you are running over a series of ten hurdles. Do the math. You can't think and hurdle at the same time.

Hurdling is instinctive. You don't think about balance, timing, when to jump, how many steps to take or anything else. You explode out of the starting blocks and run the race; that's the whole story.

Well, not exactly the whole story. There's an interesting twist to hurdling that you can see, vividly, when you know the secret. The key is to get your "lead" foot (the one that you kick over the hurdle first) back down on the ground as quickly as possible after you clear the hurdle. Competitive hurdlers call it "snapping" your lead foot back down as close to the hurdle as possible. Watch for the "snap step" the next time you see hurdlers performing.

Hurdlers know that you are getting no traction and no acceleration while your foot is in the air; the more rapidly you can return it to terra firma the better.

In the picture on the right, the position of the hurdler second from the right shows the use of the snap step. His left leg, the one that appears to be straight up and down in the picture, is his lead leg, the one that goes over the hurdle first. After clearing the hurdle, he has snapped his lead foot immediately to the track and is about to push off this foot into the next long stride.

No one "soars" over the hurdles, they step over them. Hurdlers work at this snap-step until it is, yes, *instinctive*.

What does this have to do with life after retiring? What does hurdling tell us about crafting your future? Let's look at instinct and intuition and how they can be powerful resources for you.

Instinct and Intuition

It is important to draw a distinction between two words that are sometimes (inaccurately) used interchangeably: intuition and instinct.

- Intuition has to do with *what we know*. It is a sudden insight, a "knowing" without any corroborating evidence, without any rational thought process. You don't know why you know, but you know. When we speak of "going with our gut," we are referring to intuition, to our *knowing* what is right, what the answer is, without really having our brains involved. We aren't even referring to our brains, but to our minds; not to our intestines, but to our gut. Mind and gut are metaphors for human organs; in fact, they are strategic capabilities, two of the three aforementioned centers (along with heart) of consciousness and motivation that describe how human beings operate.

- Instinct has to do with *what we do* (as opposed to intuition having to do with what we know). Instinct has the same root word as "instigate," which is a word of action, of initiating or beginning something. It is about response to a stimulus, about behavior below the conscious level. When we say that hurdling is instinctive, we mean that when you run the hurdles your body knows what it is supposed to do. When you come out of the starting blocks, your body takes over: you go over the first hurdle in stride, snap your foot down, take three steps and take the next hurdle in the same manner. Eight hurdles later, you sprint for the finish line and, hopefully, break the tape. Thinking is strictly optional. Yogi Berra was speaking a profound truth.

Let's apply this to the Decathlon Life, and let's begin by revisiting this idea developed by the ancient Greeks of the three centers of consciousness. How do these show up in modern American society; how are we taught to use these resources?

We spend our childhoods and significant amounts of our adult lives learning how to use our minds to solve problems and to get along in the world. Our schools teach us how to do this beginning in first grade or before, and continuing for as long as we stay in the educational system, sometimes for twenty years or more. Training, retraining, continuing education and certification, recertification and licensing are all part of our adult systems and procedures. On the Greek mind/heart/gut model, our society has provided many resources and institutions to help us develop the capabilities of our minds.

The idea of societal resources and institutions established to help improve our ability to use our hearts is not so well developed. We traditionally learned the lessons of the heart—of compassion, selflessness, caring and giving—from our family or from our religion, but both of these institutions are under fire today. With family ties more tenuous and religious values less espoused by our cultural institutions, we are much more on our own in developing our heart-based consciousness. Still, even in the absence of reliable training and instruction, we recognize that the heart is a powerful and valuable dimension of what makes us human.

But what do the institutions of our society, educational or otherwise, teach us about strengthening or using our "gut" tools, intuition and instinct? Precious little. In fact, it is probably not an exaggeration to say that we are given no practical instruction at all. So, did the ancient Greeks miss the point? Should we just say that humans have only two centers of power, the mind and the heart, and close up shop and go home?

Not on our watch.

Bill's Life Changes Direction

From Bill:

It was a beautiful May morning in Knoxville; I was sitting on the front steps of my house looking at the mail (they actually delivered the mail in the morning back then) while I waited to compete in a high school track meet that afternoon. It was the East Tennessee Regional Meet; the winners in each event would move on to the State Meet in Cookeville the following weekend. I was graduating in a few weeks; today would be the last time I ran on my home track.

I was excited but trying to stay calm; I was favored to win both the Regional and State Meets in the 180 yard low hurdles; I was the reigning state champ and state record holder in the event, and I had not lost a race in almost two years.

That was about to change and all because they delivered the mail in the morning.

One envelope caught my eye. It was addressed to me; it was from the University of Tennessee and it was skinny; that might be bad news. When I opened it, it contained only one page.

The letter said that I could present it to the Registrar and to the Bookstore that September; the University was awarding me an Engineering Scholarship to cover all tuition, fees and books for my freshman year.

I still remember the instant and complete change in my life. I didn't have to weigh the consequences or make a choice; it was already settled, in the blink of an eye. It was intuitive.

I was no longer a hurdler. I was an engineering student, an engineer in kit form, some assembly required.

I was a little stunned that it seemed to be such a done deal. I wasn't responsible for deciding if I wanted my life to change; it had changed.

(Continued)

(Continued)

I went out that afternoon and lost the race.

My identity had been "hurdler" for three years; I discovered as a high school sophomore that I had been given a gift; I beat the defending state champ and bettered the state record in the second race I ever ran. Prior to that time I was a nerdy, bookish kind of kid, interested in science, math and sports, in that order. With that gift, I became "somebody"—I became a hurdler.

After that great Saturday morning and tough Saturday afternoon I was able to redeem myself a week later, and I continued as a better-than-average hurdler in college, but my primary identity as a hurdler was over. It wasn't a choice; I intuitively experienced the change. It was time to grow up; to move on. My life was taking a different direction. Run fast; try to keep up.

Developing Instinct and Intuition

Just as we can develop our minds, our ability to think rationally, we can develop our instinctive and intuitive capabilities, and for the layman the process is much the same.

- We pay attention (more easily now, because we have given it a name) when our intuition tells us something about a situation, or a person, or an organization we are dealing with. We are more aware when we suspect a person's motive isn't being accurately revealed, or when we feel vaguely uneasy about a situation we find ourselves in. We may not actively respond, may not take any overt action—we may only note our intuitive powers communicating with us—but we are more aware, more conscious when we experience a certain "knowing" about a situation without any outward evidence.

- It is later that the learning begins, when we have a chance to test our "knowing" against more concrete evidence that a person in fact did have a hidden agenda, or that some pertinent fact was deliberately being withheld from us. We may find that we were wrong, that we were unduly concerned; but as we notice and trust our intuition more often, our success ratio improves and we learn to trust our gut. We have begun to develop a new resource to call upon.

- In the same way, we can begin to explore the instinctive side of human behavior; to notice the physical signs that tell us more about people and circumstances; the behavioral patterns (and deviation from patterns) that give us clues about what is going on. When you are in an animated conversation with someone, for example, and are trying to explain a complex or intricate point, you might watch for an involuntary, almost imperceptible *blink* in the eyes of your partner; this is a strong indication that the two of you are beginning to connect at a deeper, more instinctive level.

- Where have you used your instinct in your life? When have you put your body or mind on "cruise control" to finish an overtime project or defuse an awkward or dangerous situation? We suspect that the ordinary people who led their office mates down scores of flights of stairs in the Twin Towers on 9/11 were functioning on instinct. Sometimes we just know what to do.

- As we mentioned in the chapter on the Shot Put, there might be a large component of *intuition* in what we refer to as "wisdom." Our ability to intuitively know the best approach to take, even in unfamiliar situations, may have little or nothing to do with the mind. If true, this would indicate that being wise is not solely a function of the mind but depends on the development of the gut center as well.

- It would also be poetic justice if this connection between wisdom and intuition could be researched and confirmed by a grey-haired Decathlon Life participant, representing a group that might be commonly perceived to have become wise by becoming old. Life is just full of irony, isn't it?

Like those 3-D pictures of twenty years ago, the ones where we unfocused our eyes to see the three dimensional effect, developing our intuition and instinct requires us to "unfocus" what we intellectually know about a situation or a person and listen to the messages coming from our gut. We have all done it; we just didn't know it was a resource we could call on.

This is not some sort of black magic or an attempt to manipulate someone against their will; it is just an acknowledgement that the ancient Greeks were right with their model of human consciousness that included heart, mind and gut. Intuition and instinct are powerful resources and the 110 meter hurdle race is a good metaphorical (instinctive, if you will) reminder of that.

Closing Thoughts – Using the 110 Meter Hurdles

If this event, this metaphor speaks to you, it may manifest in the way you deal with your advisory board, or your spouse, or your congressman. You may discover that you have several more arrows in your quiver that you didn't know about. We think the Greeks were on to something with their three centers of heart, mind and gut; we also think it's fascinating that the culture that developed this model of human consciousness also gave us the Olympic Games; surely this is not coincidental.

Living in the Present

The three centers of human being (heart, mind, gut) are also portrayed as having different relationships with time:

- The mind center is most adept at dealing with the <u>future</u>; we have no concept or vision of the future except what we can imagine, and imagination is a function of the mind.

- The heart center is most associated with the <u>past</u>; we get our values from our lifetime experiences and we are told that our emotions are most often triggered and constrained by our past.

- Our gut center, where our intuition and instinct live, is most associated with our <u>present</u>, with our here and now. It is characterized by how our bodies respond to stimuli of all sorts, known as a "gut reaction."

This may explain why we have such difficulty listening to others in a conversation, why we must be exhorted to "be here now." We don't often live in the present. We have little or no training and very few distinctions around developing our ability to *be present*. We seriously short-change ourselves in this area.

Maybe you will change that. We're pulling for you.

CHAPTER 10

DEFINING THE DECATHLON LIFE

What is the Decathlon Life, exactly? How do you define it?

Beats us.

It is a little embarrassing to write a book about something you have no definition for. Until you realize that the reason it is undefined is the whole point.

We mentioned earlier that we believe that innovations and changes work best when they are initiated from points toward the bottom of the society hierarchy rather than from the top. The first practical airplane design was developed by two brothers in a bicycle shop, not in the 1903 equivalent of the Pentagon. How would you define the "Decathlon Lives" the Wright brothers lived? Who cares about a definition?

Well, okay, we'll give it a try: the Decathlon Life participant is engaged, resourceful, motivated, attentive, faster than a speeding bullet, able to leap tall buildings, etc....unless they're not. People come in all models, and Decathlon Life practitioners are just people.

There are potentially 10,000 new Decathlon Life journeys beginning every day—and you want a *definition*?

Perhaps we could say that the Decathlon Life is about beginnings, dreams and craftsmanship—and sometimes even about the unsung hero, the hero next door.

Beginnings

Human beings are far more inclined to celebrate beginnings than endings. The signing of the Declaration of Independence on July 4, 1776, was the beginning of a great experiment, but few people recall the date at the end of the War for American Independence when the British agreed to give the young United States its freedom. Similarly, the attack on Pearl Harbor on December 7, 1941 will be forever remembered as the date of our entry into World War II, but who remembers the date that the peace treaties were signed in Tokyo Bay?

We are a people of beginnings, not endings.

But those of us in our 50's, 60's, and 70's are planning for, or living into, that part of our lives called "retirement." Society tells us it's too late for us, too late for another beginning or two or three.

We don't buy it for a minute.

Both authors of this book have fond memories of being part of notable beginnings. Betty was a forerunner of the emergence in American society of women as leaders, as innovators, as trend setters. She was part of an unbroken string of "First woman…" accomplishments. First woman dean, first woman president, first woman board member, first woman chairperson and on and on. Bill, working for IBM, was in on the beginning of automating business processes in manufacturing organizations in the 1960s and became an internal IBM resource. He was part of the generation that defined the mainframe computer revolution. He still talks of the days of "making it up as we went along."

Beginnings are far more energizing and fulfilling than endings. Endings are about memories of the past; beginnings are about dreams of the future. It seems to us that our society, our nation, our world needs people with dreams of the future.

But what are dreams anyway? It might be a good idea to look at that question.

Dreams

In our hyper-pragmatic world, we can be chided for admitting to dreams. Manipulative marketing firms can create misleading advertising touting a "dream vacation," or a "dream house," but we big boys and girls know that this is all bull feathers. The dictionary defines a *dreamer* as:

- ...one who lives in a world of fantasy and imagination, or
- ...one who has ideas or conceives projects regarded as impractical.

Thank goodness we are beyond that, right? Thank goodness our culture is far too mature and sophisticated to be swayed by *dreams*! Just say no to impractical ideas and projects!

Well, perhaps dreams are just waiting for the proper time to appear.

Dreams and Visions

Almost 3000 years ago, the God of the Hebrews spoke through the prophet Joel:

...your sons and daughters shall prophesy; your old men shall dream dreams, your young men shall see visions.

– Joel 2:28

Or, perhaps dreams are waiting for the proper spokespeople. Of course, the male retirees can be referred to, as in the Biblical reference, as "old men," while the female retirees are more properly referred to as "Ladies of Maturity and Wisdom."

The terms dreams and visions are sometimes used interchangeably, but there seems to be a subtle difference, and the aforementioned advertising mavens have discovered it: dreams carry a connotation of quality, of excellence, that visions do not. No one longs for "vision vacations" or "vision houses."

So dreams are to be valued, and we of the weathered countenance are to be their bearers. Well, we can handle that. But let's not forget the second part of Joel's prophecy: ...*your young men shall see visions.*

Dreams are not enough; we need visions and plans, something that people can see and understand, and our young men and women, visionaries that they are, have a feel for the current culture and its mores that we will never be able to match. Link up with the younger generation; we need each other's perspective. Merge our dreams with their visions.

The decathlon is a young person's sport; it requires prodigious quantities of energy, strength and endurance. But competing in the decathlon, which demands that you perform at your absolute best, can also generate energy, can create new strength, and can increase endurance. It is these reservoirs of new energy, new strength and new endurance that you can tap into when you are creating new beginnings, when you begin to craft your Decathlon Life, but don't underestimate the power of dreams...

> Row, row, row your boat
> Gently down the stream
> Merrily, merrily, merrily, merrily
> Life is but a dream.

And with that, let's spend a moment on craftsmanship.

Craftsmanship

When we speak of crafting a future or a life, we are not being flippant. Sometimes, as you may already have discovered, we enjoy being flippant, so it's best if we distinguish those times when we definitely are not.

Considering how life works, the future is all that we have any control over. We certainly can't change the past—it has *passed*, after all, which is how it got its name—and while we can choose how we react or respond to the present, we can't change it.

But we can change our future. We have a great deal of influence over how the future shows up, in our lives and the lives of those we touch.

And not only can we change our future, we can craft it. There is artistry, creativity and imagination in craftsmanship.

But associated with the individual craftsman there is an instinctive talent, an inborn strength, a force of boldness and confidence that is straining to be released, surging to express its uniqueness; what it was created to do and be. This is the craft, the art, almost separate from the craftsman but not quite. This is the music that plays the musician rather than vice versa, the dance that spins and leaps the dancer into ever more unbelievable, gravity-defying moves.

This is what the craftsman was born to do, the talent they were destined to contribute. For this they came. They contribute, and they are fulfilled. It is just that simple.

And their craft might be spending an afternoon, twice a week, with an autistic child, serving and drinking imaginary tea, helping to heal a mis-wired mind. It might be sorting through donated clothes at a thrift shop, not as an onerous task, but as a way to help restore health and dignity to someone, or several someones, who are down on their luck.

Or it might be serving in Congress. There are no creative limits or age limits on craftsmanship.

Betty looks at where the Decathlon Life might lead:

The Hero Next Door

In 1982, *Time* magazine's "Man of the Year" was a machine: the Computer. Surely there must have been someone—a human being, I mean—more deserving of the title.

My choice that year would have been the man in the water in the Air Florida 90 crash.

On January 13, 1982, an Air Florida plane hit the Potomac River bridge (ice had formed on the wings), landed in the water and began to sink. Television cameras picked up the few survivors clinging to the aircraft's tail as hovering helicopters dropped rescue rings into the water.

One man reached for the ring, pulled it to himself, and then gave it to someone else. Another came down, and again he grabbed it and gave it away. Again and again, he gave the ring away.

Finally the ring came for him; he was the last one on the tail of the plane. He reached up to grab the ring, hesitated, pulled it to himself, drew himself out of the water, but he was too chilled by the cold, too diminished by his efforts to save the others, and he couldn't manage to pull himself into the ring. He slid below the waters and drowned before our very eyes. Television caught it all.

He appeared to be an ordinary man...a burly, balding, mustached man. He was an ordinary man who did an extraordinary thing. When I think of him, I think of Joseph Campbell's "Hero With a Thousand Faces." That is what heroes are: ordinary people doing extraordinary things.

Thirty years ago we were younger and life was simpler, or seems to have been in retrospect. The world has changed in those thirty years, but we suspect that human beings change on a very different time scale.

We think there are still heroes walking our planet; quite a few of them, actually. Not many of their deeds will be captured on television but we'll bet those heroic deeds occur quite frequently and perhaps only one or two people notice, or they may go unnoticed all together. We all have chances to make life a little easier, a little nicer for those around us.

This book has been written for the unsung, unnoticed, unidentified heroes among us; the ordinary people doing things which to the world might appear to be ordinary but in fact are quite extraordinary.

People like you.

THE HIGH JUMP

CHAPTER 11

THE HIGH JUMP

Imagination

> **Just Imagine...**
>
> When we have committed to accomplishing something important to us, when we have identified our strengths and expanded our boundaries, when we become the beginner again, when we explore our intuition and instinct...
>
> Whole new vistas just might begin to open up.
>
> Use your imagination: what in the world could you do now?
>
> Meet Dick Fosbury who at age fifteen reinvented the High Jump.

People who see competitive high jumping for the first time can't believe their eyes.

Decades ago, high jumpers used a sort of "scissors kick." Competitors ran a few yards to build momentum, approached running parallel to the bar, then kicked their lead leg and then their trailing leg over the bar, landing on their feet on the other side.

When sawdust pits were added, allowing the jumpers a cushioned landing, the "Western Roll" became popular. The jumpers, still running parallel to the bar, would launch themselves into the air, kicking their trailing leg first, in such a way that they were facing downward when they cleared the bar, and literally "rolled" into the pit, usually cushioning their fall with their arms and legs. Using this technique, the participants significantly raised the winning heights and high jump records fell.

When You Least Expect It

Then, in the mid-sixties, two phenomena appeared simultaneously: deeper, more cushioned high jump pits and Dick Fosbury. Fosbury was a tall, thin teenaged high jumper in Medford, Oregon when sawdust high jump pits began to be replaced with foam rubber pits, which made the chance of injury much less risky. Fosbury began experimenting at the age of fifteen with a new technique which was revolutionary: rather than jumping while running parallel to the bar, Fosbury's approach saw him launching his jump while facing away from the bar and going over the bar and into the pit backwards and head first, looking not toward the ground but toward the sky, finally landing in the pit on the back of his head and shoulders. A thing of beauty it was not.

Needless to say, it was a time of trial and error since he had no mentor to teach him (he was making it up as he went along). He was terribly inconsistent at first, but he kept experimenting and honing his style and then he began to win a few meets.

Fosbury continued to work on the technique during his college years at Oregon State University; he was winning meets but not winning any imitators. A wiseacre newspaper reporter dubbed his technique the "Fosbury Flop," saying it looked like a fish flopping in the bottom of a boat.

Fosbury had the last laugh. In 1968, at the age of twenty-one, he won the National Collegiate Athletic Association championship, won the U.S. Olympic Trials and set a new Olympic record at the 1968 Games in Mexico City, looking good at last as he stood proudly on the podium to receive the gold medal.

He received the ultimate compliment when competitors began to copy his revolutionary technique.

The superiority of his methodology was so complete that four years later, at the 1972 Olympic Games in Munich, twenty-eight of the forty competitors used the "Flop"; indeed, from the 1972 Olympics through the 2000 Olympics, twenty-one of the twenty-four medalists in the high jump used Dick Fosbury's jumping style.

Sometimes looking good is overrated.

Following the Leader or Becoming the Leader

There are lessons to be learned and life metaphors to be explored by examining Dick Fosbury's courageous path to changing the way an international sport is conducted. Can you imagine the lonely feeling of being the only competitor to use such an ungainly looking style? At age fifteen, or seventeen, or twenty, can you imagine how easy it would have been to merely start doing it like everyone else? Can you imagine how many times his friends, teammates, coaches, and even his family had to struggle to be loyal in the face of cascading disagreement and doubt? Even today, the style does not get many points for beauty.

But every winner uses it.

Practical and Impractical Applications

We propose several approaches that may prove to be helpful as you apply the story of Dick Fosbury's courage to your own journey, the crafting of your Decathlon Life:

- Use your imagination. Innovate. Be creative in noticing how your world is showing up in your life. Be aware of circumstances changing, of new opportunities emerging. If you have a better idea, if deeper high jump pits allow for different techniques, go with your instincts and invent a new style. Huddle with your advisory board to get their feedback, but lean toward the bold approach. Let others worry about looking good.

- The key is to keep on top of what is changing in your immediate world. New regulations may give you a new opportunity to help others cope with new requirements; a new product may make your services more valuable or the need for them more apparent; new information sources may give you a new way to connect with your target audience.

- Change how you do things. Change directions, change approaches, change procedures, change priorities. Remember that Dick Fosbury changed the direction of his approach to the bar; perhaps you should change the direction of your approach to your project.

- Don't be afraid to acknowledge that you have been handling things the old way when a new way, even if it looks funny for a while, might give surprising results. See what you can incorporate and/or salvage from your efforts up till now, and focus your energy on a different path for the future.

- Question "best practices." You don't know what assumptions were made when those practices were deemed "best." Maybe the practices you invented would be better, fresher, or more creative. Maybe things have changed. Maybe they overlooked your experience and wisdom. You are the craftsman of your unique future; you get to design it the way you want it to look.

- Have fun while you innovate. Ultimately, you are motivated by doing what you enjoy doing. As you craft your Decathlon Life, you are the only one you have to answer to, so do things your way and have a good time.

- Don't be afraid to look different, even humorous. It takes a big person to poke fun at themselves and people instinctively respect this. Opening yourself to share humor with another person can be an act of intimacy and can deepen trust that flows both ways in a relationship.

- When everything is working, bring innovation to bear by putting your own personal stamp on it; tapping into your dream, your vision; crafting what you want it all to look like when you reach your goal. How could you shorten the time to have it all work? How do you use the power of the future to give you energy and commitment in the present? How do you harness your instinct, your gut feelings, your sense of what is coming? Betty quotes Wayne Gretzky, the ice hockey immortal: "I don't skate to the puck. I skate to where the puck is going to be."

That is mastery. That is artistry. That is craftsmanship.

You can do it.

Being Big Enough to Be Different

From Bill:

Betty has a flair for being accessible, inspirational and unpredictable. There is a booth named in her honor (complete with engraved plaque) at the Waffle House near the Kennesaw State University (KSU) campus where she was President for twenty-five years. She ate breakfast there on a regular basis; any student could sit in her booth and talk with her about any subject—no appointment needed. She took notes on the Waffle House napkins and if a student named a particularly effective professor, Betty wrote that professor with congratulations and a note that their next Waffle House breakfast was on her.

(Continued)

(Continued)

When on-campus housing was added at KSU, President Betty spent dozens of nights in the Women's Dormitory, wearing her fuzzy slippers, playing cards, watching television, listening first hand to the concerns and suggestions of the students. She often said that she wanted KSU to be a "value added" university, one that met the emotional needs as well as the educational needs of the students.

During the Atlanta Olympics of 1996, Betty was Chair of the Atlanta Chamber of Commerce, a member of the President's Representatives for the Games and carried the Olympic torch for a segment of its journey through the city streets on the way to the stadium. She was intensely proud of being a member of the Organizing Committee for the Special Olympics, held in Atlanta shortly after the larger event concluded.

Betty has always been a pace setter, in community life as well as in the field of higher education, but she also carries the torch for those who are big enough to listen to the beginners, who are not afraid to look different and sometimes even funny in order to show, down deep, how alike we all are.

THE JAVELIN

CHAPTER 12

THE JAVELIN

Leverage

Ancient and Modern Leverage

Now you are cooking. During the start phase of your project, you were getting up to speed from a standing (crouching, in the 100 meters) start; this took a lot of energy for pretty meager results. Now you are expending a lot less energy and achieving better results, more sustaining power, and greater personal fulfillment.

Now is the time to use the resources around you; your contacts, your networks, your associations, your vision. It is time to work smarter, not harder.

It is time to use *leverage*.

And, of course, leverage brings us to the Javelin!

The javelin throw is one of the Decathlon's most *beautiful* events. The long, soaring arc that the javelin traces across the sky can lift the spirit, engage the heart, and please the eyes.

It was not always so.

113

In ancient Greece, the javelin throwers were the artillery of their day; they were the long range guns. The sight of javelins coming their way did not lift spirits but generated dread in the troops on the receiving end; javelins were designed to rain death and destruction on an enemy force from a distance.

The javelin throw, along with the discus, long jump and a variation of the 100 meter dash, is one of the modern decathlon events which have their roots in the Olympic Games of ancient Greece. A warrior who could throw for distance and accuracy, who could send a javelin deep into the enemy's battle formations, would receive rewards on the battlefield and fame every four years in the Games.

The benign descendant of those ancient battles has morphed into a modern athletic event of beauty and grace; one which requires strength, accuracy and agility, and a healthy measure of foot speed.

In modern competition, men's javelins are about eight feet long and weigh a little less than two pounds. To throw the javelin, competitors run along a twelve-foot wide 100 foot long runway and, without crossing an arc marked on the ground, throw the javelin with an overhand motion. The curved arc extends forward into a twenty-nine degree sector, or area; only throws landing within this sector are measured. World class athletes can launch throws that travel 100 yards (300 feet), the length of a football field. The javelin is the decathlon's longest throwing event.

The "run up" (when the competitor builds momentum, running toward the launch point) has its own form of beauty. As the athlete's speed increases and they begin to cock their arm to throw, it is not difficult to imagine the warriors on ancient battlefields executing the same regimen.

The Value of Leverage

The javelin provided a degree of *leverage* to the Greek warriors:

- Throwing the weapon into the air toward a distant enemy gave at least theoretical safety to the thrower, as opposed to a warrior who carried a spear and engaged in hand-to-hand fighting. This was the principle of effect at a distance.

- A javelin launched into the air and following a ballistic path would be travelling faster and with more momentum when it returned to earth; this was the principle of multiplying our physical strength.

Leverage

The word leverage is, of course, derived from the word lever, which was one of the three "simple machines" (the others were the pulley and the screw) identified by the Greek mathematician/engineer Archimedes in the third century BCE. Archimedes did not invent the lever, but he famously said, "Give me a place to stand and a lever and I will move the earth." While in retrospect this seems a magnificently safe boast to make, it does illustrate the power and antiquity of the lever—and conveniently, places it as a contemporary of the ancient Olympic Games.

Leverage is a multiplier of power. You take your car to a repair shop and the mechanic puts a jack under the axle of the car and pumps on a long handle to lift your car off the ground. The mechanic is using leverage. He pumps the handle through an arc of several feet, but with each cycle your car is raised only a fraction of an inch. The mechanic can't lift the car with his arms, but by using the lever (and leverage) he multiplies his own physical strength and raises the heavy car.

In living the Decathlon Life, we are not looking for ways to increase our physical strength, but ways of increasing our impact on the world around us. This in turn increases our ability to influence our own personal future and potentially the future of our community. Leverage enables us to:

- Multiply our impact through what we do and what we enroll others to do with us.

- Affect communities and societies beyond our ability to physically interact with them through our connections with people in those places.

- Craft our own unique future and establish ways to sustain what we begin.

Leverage and the IBM Salesperson/Consultant

When Bill joined IBM in 1966, all commercial computers were mainframe computers and only the largest of organizations had them. IBM had eighty percent of the US marketplace and it was the mission of the IBM sales force to expand computer ownership into a broader base of large and medium sized organizations—businesses, hospitals, universities, governments, wherever—to bring the world into the computer age.

It was an interesting time. There were few computer programming classes available, even at the university level, and none available to the general public. When IBM sold computers to customers it was with the assurance that the IBM engineers and programmers would design and write the programs for the customer to use, and it was all part of the price of the machine. It required a significant amount of faith and trust on the part of the decision maker to turn all of this over to an outside vendor, even one as large as IBM. Sometimes that faith and trust was slow in coming.

But IBM had a secret weapon: Executive Education. This was IBM's leverage system, its javelin.

In a dozen or so Executive Centers around the country and soon even more around the world, IBM offered intensive week-long courses in how to understand and

(Continued)

(Continued)

utilize large, centralized computers. These courses were free but were offered by invitation only, and invitations were restricted to the top two or three people in an organization: the President, Executive Vice President, and maybe the Chief Financial Officer.

The IBM course instructors taught the history of computers, explained how their design had evolved, and talked of how various industries and organizations had adapted them for their specific use. They provided details on how the best computer departments were organized, how other companies (with IBM's help) had designed and installed their corporate systems, and what kinds of financial benefits they were experiencing. The instructors, all former engineers and salespeople themselves, conducted a seminar on what the future looked like and what worked to get you there.

The IBM instructors showed how computer designs were evolving and improving and suggested how an organization might plan for the expansion and evolution of a central computer facility as their requirements grew. They discussed IBM's plans for future technology developments and how that might affect new automation possibilities in each industry segment.

Throughout the week, the instructors stressed that IBM wanted to be a partner, not a vendor; that IBM's success depended entirely on the success of their customers—those same customers that were in the room. In the days of the "high magic" 1960s computer landscape, it was a reassuring and empowering message.

IBM even taught the executives to write programs in two different computer "languages." How could you "know" and fully utilize a computer until you could speak its language?

Imagine if you will, a team made up of a hospital chief administrator, the president of a bank and the owner of a

(Continued)

(Continued)

string of car dealerships working late into the night to get their COBOL program to accurately calculate the current wealth of the Native Americans who sold Manhattan Island to the Dutch if they had invested their money at five percent interest. The teamwork between the executives often produced life changing experiences.

At the end of the week, the executives would return to their organizations with a new sense of confidence and the beginnings of a game plan to take their people into the digital age. They also had the names and phone numbers of a couple dozen other decision makers that they now knew as friends and as people they could trust for advice and counsel in a fast-moving digital world.

And oh, by the way, they had an appointment the following week with the IBM Marketing Representative who enrolled them in the class, a young man or woman with the same capabilities and experiences as their course instructors, and one whom they were beginning to think of as a consultant rather than as a sales person.

That is why IBM had eighty percent of the marketplace.

That is leverage.

Relationships as Leverage

Nothing quite separates and polarizes people who work in organizations like the subject of teams. Some people depend on teams, others shudder at the thought of them. Organizational consultants build whole industries around team building exercises, seminars, retreats. The score at the end of the day: some people like to work on teams, others prefer to work alone. You probably know which camp you are in.

A lot of people retiring from a career in organizations might choose to never serve on a team again. The concept of relationships-as-leverage is bad news for these folks. On the other hand, leverage is accomplishing things at a distance; multiplying your power. This is why people form teams: to do things you can't do alone.

Leverage in the Decathlon Life scheme of things doesn't require you to organize a team or even to be a member of a team. Perhaps you could arrange for a team to engage in an activity, or enroll the team members or their leaders in something you want to happen.

Suppose you enrolled the New York Mets baseball players in dressing up as Santa Claus and visiting city fire departments and police stations where the staff can't be at home on Christmas, and you even enroll the Mets administration in handling all the logistics. Think of how you might be able to leverage your relationship with the Mets—and the police and fire fighters—in the future.

There are people in our communities who could use some help from an organization, and there are organizations that are looking for ways to be good corporate citizens. Getting the two together can be a fulfilling challenge. And you don't have to work on a team; it's the relationship that provides the leverage, not the team.

The Advantage of a Prominent Place

On the battlefields of the ancient world, competing armies that could gain the high ground (a hill or ridge) would have a huge advantage because of the greater range provided to their javelin throwers. Then as now, a place of prominence, a place of higher elevation, offered warriors two significant advantages:

- Their range was increased because they were throwing down hill. In addition, the opposing javelin throwers were at a significant disadvantage for the opposite reason; they were throwing toward a target above them.

- The warriors atop the hill also had a superior view of the battlefield; they could more accurately pick their targets.

The Prominent Place and the Decathlon Life

Throwing from a place of prominence multiplied the leverage of the ancient javelin thrower; having access to a place of prominence can multiply the impact and influence of the person living the Decathlon Life as well.

What might this place of prominence look like? Pick one or more from the following list:

- You are known in your community; people listen when you speak. ("Community" can be defined as the world, your own neighborhood, or somewhere in between.)

- You are a leader, an organizer; people follow you; leading is what you do best.

- You can enroll people in your passion, your ideas; they sign on to your vision.

- You understand and can use modern technology and social media.

- You can recruit and inspire people who have the qualifications listed above.

Working from a place of prominence will not appeal to everyone. This illustrates one of the most important features of the Decathlon Life: there are no rules, no best practices, and no school solutions. *You* are crafting your own unique future; you have only yourself to answer to.

But if you do choose, as the ancient javelin throwers did, to work from a place of prominence, you will find your efforts, your impact, and your influence will be multiplied dramatically.

In addition, your view is improved as well – not of the battlefield, but of the future. Because you are leveraging your strengths with the strengths of others, you have the clarity and vision of a team, not of a single individual.

And you are not limited to *seeing* your future—you can create it. Even craft it.

Where can you make your javelin fly?

Betty's Life of Leverage

From Bill:

Betty Siegel has been impacting the society around her for decades, and we sometimes forget the social circumstances that existed when she began shaking up the academic world.

I joined IBM in 1966 and was amazed to find that my first sales training class in New York City consisted of about twenty males and about a dozen females. I had been in the business world for six years and had only encountered a handful of female professionals. The previous year, working for Procter and Gamble in Chicago, I had attended a management development course along with managers from other companies such as Sears and Chevron; the 100 or so participants were all male.

For a great look at how petrified our gender assumptions had become, watch the 1967 movie *How to Succeed in Business Without Really Trying*. In the movie, the career path for business women was from the typing pool to secretary. Period.

Into this barren desert of opportunity comes Betty, wearing her husband's clothes (see Chapter 15) and over time, wearing down the traditional gender assumptions.

She didn't march in the streets (well, she did carry the Olympic torch on its journey, if that counts) or write articles or give speeches in support of women's rights, she took the hard road: she went to work in the innermost bastions of male superiority, rolled up her sleeves and did the same work that they were doing—except a little better than they were doing it.

(Continued)

(Continued)

This is what I found when I worked shoulder to shoulder with the women in that first IBM sales training class: on average, they were a little sharper and more competent than the men. And this was not a casual observation; that first class was ten weeks long, and there was about a 20 percent drop-out rate. It was not a walk in the park.

I had an advantage in being able to judge the women honestly: I came from a region, the Appalachian area of East Tennessee, where women were expected to be strong. These were the descendants of the pioneers who crossed these mountains and cleared out these forests back in the 1700s. The women were equal partners with the men in those days because nobody could claim the convenience of being fragile.

When your nearest neighbors are eight miles away, you do whatever needs to be done to survive; whatever you have the strength to do. I was raised by strong women and lived around strong women and it was not a problem for me to welcome them in as equals.

Interestingly enough, Betty came from a similar region, the Appalachians of Eastern Kentucky. What a surprise.

So Betty began to change things, always making friends, defusing conflicts, being helpful and patient. But doing things a little better than the men did them—quietly, casually, and consistently.

She began to leverage her talents and skills in two distinct ways:

- For the men who were paying attention, she demonstrated that women could not only successfully carry their own weight, but could bring a whole new dimension, a new balance, a new perspective to a hitherto exclusive boys club. It was a winning combination. A bit of the woman's touch, if you will.

(Continued)

(Continued)

- For the women, who definitely were paying attention, she served not only as a role model but as a demonstration that the glass ceiling was breaking up. Committed women could aim for bigger and better things, could begin to extend their boundaries. We see today the benefit of Betty's sea change, but it was not that obvious forty years ago.

Betty's leverage has extended beyond the arena of gender issues. When she took the reins at Kennesaw State College in 1981, it was generally regarded as a community college, with no residence dormitories and an average student age of twenty-seven. Today it has grown 600 percent since 1981 and is considered among the national leaders in several programs. Most significantly, however, it has developed an eclectic relationship with its community.

Cobb County has grown to become, arguably, Georgia's most influential county. KSU has been an important part of that growth. Betty's leverage has been seen in both camps:

- Betty demonstrated to students that they could learn about values and character as well as prepare for a career. Her promotion of "Rock Solid Values" (named for Remembrance Rock, a campus icon popularized by Betty) led to the establishment of the *Siegel Institute for Leadership, Ethics, and Character*, an internationally-known organization sponsored by the University and by committed individuals within the community.

- She demonstrated to the University's host community that graduates who are exposed to the conversation about these values became more solid citizens and contribute positively to the strength and character of the community in which they live. The University has become a powerful influence for increased community development and growth.

(Continued)

> *(Continued)*
>
> Betty's life of applying leverage at just the right time and in just the right way has had exceptional impact. Oh, by the way, the javelin event is about to begin and they are calling your name...

CHAPTER 13

FEAR OF FAILURE

Consider the neophyte decathlon athlete.

Chances are, you are pretty good, maybe very good, at five, six, or even seven of the ten decathlon events. Let's say you are a world-class javelin thrower, a great high jumper and long jumper, a decent pole vaulter, and competitive in the 100 and 400 meters.

Now you have to deal with the 110 meter hurdles, the shot put, discus and the 1500 meters. You have to develop the skills in these events to compete with the best athletes in the world.

Can you see where that might be a challenging future?

What Is Failure?

What is failure for a decathlon athlete? Is it knocking the bar off in pole vaulting?

It happens for every pole vault competitor in every match; it is a guaranteed outcome in every competition (unless you quit early). The end of the event comes when the last competitor knocks the bar off on their third attempt. But the last height that the vaulter cleared might have established a new world record. Is their subsequent inability to clear a greater height to be considered a *failure*? Of course not; they are the new world record holder. They are the most successful pole vaulter of all time.

In head-to-head pole vault competition (non-decathlon) the last competitor to knock the bar off for the last time is awarded the gold medal. This is certainly not failure.

Is losing the race failure? The last event in decathlon competition is the 1500 meters run, and like all the other events, you are running against the clock. If you finish in 4:25 (four minutes and twenty-five seconds) you score a certain number of points—say 870. As a competitor in the 1500 meters, your 4:25 time might place you number eight out of a field of sixteen, but because your cumulative point total was ahead of everyone else's cumulative score, you needed only 800 points to win the ten-event decathlon. You finished eighth in the 1500 meters but won the overall competition and the gold medal. Surely this is not failure.

Is it failure when you throw the javelin 278 feet, beating your previous best of 271 feet—but you finish third in the javelin competition to other competitors with throws of 281 and 279 feet? In our judgment, this is not failure. You have surpassed your previous best. This is what the decathlon is about. Your exemplary performance, your new personal record, is a huge victory; it is your incentive to continue to improve.

The decathlon athlete lives with "failure" every day. When your best javelin throw was 278 feet, you had two other throws that day of less than 278 feet. That's why you get three throws. No one looks at these other two throws as failure. They are part of the game, part of the path of progress, part of developing your talent.

Betty is fond of saying we don't know what to fear:

In our country we fear the wrong things. We ought to fear cigarette smoke because 400,000 people a year die from inhaling cigarette smoke. We ought to fear automobile accidents. 36,000 people a year are killed in auto accidents. You know what we really fear in this country? Sharks! To prove the point all you have to do is go to the ocean, stand in the shallow water and yell "Shark!" Everybody jumps out of the water, runs to their car, and lights up a cigarette!

What is Failure in Our Lives?

Behavioral scientists tell us that what holds us back the most is a fear of failure. We suspect that we could take some lessons from the decathlon competitors. Perhaps we are making the mistake of defining our halting steps on the path of progress, our inconsistencies in the process of developing our talents, as *failures*.

Perhaps we are shrinking back when we first knock off the bar.

Perhaps we are forgetting that we may be up against competitors who are further along in the development process.

Perhaps we don't realize that we have three throws, or three jumps, and maybe many more, and that only the longest one or the highest one counts.

Life is an unbroken string of learning experiences. We fail only when we choose not to play.

The Insidious Fear

If there is one thing that might hold a decathlon athlete back, it is one that sneaks up on us all: not the fear of failing, but the fear of *succeeding*.

It is the fear that we try to ignore, that we try to label with some other name: we don't want others to look bad; we quit while we are ahead; we don't want to rub it in; we don't want to stand out in the crowd, we don't like the spotlight.

What we are often trying to ignore is our *gift*; that part of us that truly defines our exceptionality; that extraordinary strength or talent that we can contribute to the world; our unique piece that only we can place in the mosaic called life. It has nothing to do with winning, or losing, or trying to show someone else up, or feeling like we are better than them. It is all about participating, about stepping out onto the playing field.

If you have enrolled in the Decathlon Life, you are a player, you are one of the engaged. You will not fail unless you choose not to play. We're rooting for you.

THE POLE VAULT

CHAPTER 14

THE POLE VAULT

Perspective and Inspiration

Putting It All in Perspective

Now the wind is in your sails; you are actively creating your future. You are consistently living the life you have chosen to live, with all its wrinkles and wonders.

Now may be the time to ponder the impact you are having on the world around you. Now may be when you put it all in perspective.

And have you ever thought about the profound metaphorical experience that is the Pole Vault?

The pole vault deserves to be in the decathlon; it holds the prestigious position of being track and field's *highest* event. Pole vault competitors, under their own power, soar two stories (twenty feet) into the air to go over a bar suspended between two vertical standards, and they do it feet first and looking back the way they came. This is quite a feat and certainly worthy of our respect.

There are an exceptional number of athletic skills that must be already present or rigorously developed if one is to become an accomplished pole vaulter.

- You must have or develop the foot speed necessary to build momentum as you race down the runway carrying the pole toward the takeoff point. Many pole vaulters are former sprinters who have added upper-body strength and gymnastics skills.

- You must develop the timing and mental discipline that enables you to arrive at the "box" (the metal box in the ground where you place the pole) without breaking stride or losing your momentum.

- You must develop accuracy and consistency in planting the flexible pole into the box so that it bends at just the right time and at just the right angle to give you maximum lift in your vault.

- You must have or develop exceptional muscular strength to enable you to swing your body upward (you are still facing the bar at this point) until you are looking skyward and have your feet pointed into the air. See picture at right.

- You must have or develop the agility and timing of a gymnast because while still ascending you must twist your body so that the apogee of your vault carries you to the point where you are soaring over the bar and looking down the length of the pole toward the ground.

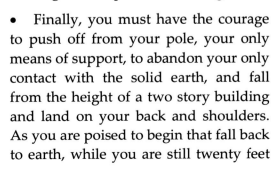

- Finally, you must have the courage to push off from your pole, your only means of support, to abandon your only contact with the solid earth, and fall from the height of a two story building and land on your back and shoulders. As you are poised to begin that fall back to earth, while you are still twenty feet in the air, you must have the feather touch to gently nudge the pole away from the bar because if it continues to move forward after you release it, the pole may knock the bar off even after your body has successfully cleared it.

Piece of cake.

Energy Conversion and the Pole Vault

The pole vault is a beautiful event to watch, with the quick changes in the participants' direction and orientation unfolding for each vault. The physics of the pole vault require the participant to convert horizontal energy (sprinting down the runway carrying the pole) into vertical energy (rising up on the flexing pole to soar over the bar), and observing this energy conversion can be fascinating.

The horizontal-to-vertical shift is a relatively common energy conversion for machines, but somewhat unique for human beings. If we look closely, we can detect a very powerful metaphor for those of us engaging in the Decathlon Life.

A lot of life is mundane, routine, ordinary; brushing our teeth and taking out the trash. Think of the everyday stuff as the "horizontal" dimension of life. As Winston Churchill once observed, "Life is just one damned thing after another."

We can also think of another dimension of life, a vertical dimension, expressed beautifully by Tuptim, the primary wife/consort to the King of Siam in the Broadway musical and movie *The King and I*. The King (played by Yul Brynner) was portrayed as emotional, dictatorial, and hard to live with. Tuptim softened this view of him by singing these lyrics:

He will not always say

What you would have him say

But now and then he'll say

Something

Wonderful.[3]

Life can be like that. Not always what we want, or expect, or welcome. But now and then, something wonderful.

Perspective

The choreography of the pole vault involves a rapid buildup of momentum; a sudden energy conversion from horizontal to vertical; another physical conversion from looking upward to looking down, from looking forward to looking back. At the top, success, or a near miss, but either way you have for an instant released your reliance on safety; you have surrendered your connection with the earth. You are soaring free, bound for earth again of course, but for a moment you have touched the sky.

This is the message of the perspective delivered by the pole vault: rise above the mundane, the uninteresting; seize the opportunity to create; convert the horizontal energy into vertical energy, into something potentially wonderful. This is not a guarantee for success; as in pole vaulting, misses can and will come, but even the near misses can be exhilarating.

Converting Horizontal Energy to Vertical Energy

Very few decathletes excel at the pole vault, but all must develop competence in the event if they intend to be competitive in international meets. Vaulting is not easy to master, but for some it can be an instinctive event. It requires understanding and mastering that one little trick, that one horizontal-vertical conversion process, when mundane becomes wonderful.

The pole vault can show us how this conversion might take place in ordinary life; how a change in perspective can convert horizontal, mundane tasks into vertical, wonderful experiences.

We propose that it happens in the domain of inspiration.

---

[3] Oscar Hammerstein II, "Something Wonderful" from *The King and I: The Complete Lyrics of Oscar Hammerstein II*, Amy Asch, Editor (New York: Alfred A. Knopf, 2008)

Inspiration

When the European languages were first coming into being, to *inspire* literally meant to *breathe*, or to breathe *into*. It shared a root word with *spirit*, which meant breath. "Inspire" and "spirit" were words used to discuss giving life to something; the act of bringing something to life, of *breathing life* into something—or someone.

People today are "brought to life" when they are inspired. People are not inspired by the mundane, the uninteresting, the ordinary; they are inspired by the special, by the wonderful; by the experience of surrendering their connection with the earth and by touching the sky; by changing the orientation of their energy from horizontal to vertical. They want to abandon the status quo; to reach above and beyond their limits; to defy gravity. The pole vault speaks of that life-giving transformation.

But not every day, not all the time, not 24/7. We want to be inspired, lifted up; but we want some degree of routine in our lives also. That's why pep rallies are only held once a week.

That's why the pole vault is just one of ten events.

Even when we pole vault, we return to earth.

Being Inspired, Being Inspirational

We have probably all been inspired by someone at one time or another, but now the challenge is issued: what would it mean for *us* to be inspirational, to inspire others, to be an inspiration?

First of all, a sure way to fail at being inspirational is to decide we are going to be inspirational. People are highly suspect of someone who declares they are inspiring. If we are inspiring, they will usually recognize it all by themselves (particularly if we are inspiring them to do something they want to do but are afraid to do).

So how do we start the horizontal-vertical energy conversion process? How do we at least begin to consider being an inspiration to someone else?

We propose that we begin by being inspired by someone or something else.

We define it as giving serious attention to something *bigger than we are.*

Inspiration in Action

When Betty introduces this story in a speech, she begins by asking "How many of you have ever cheated? Put your hands up. Now, keep them up. The rest of you, look at these people. They cheat. The rest of you, you lie."

Miss Huff Inspires a Fourth Grade Girl

When I was in the fourth grade, everybody agreed I was a good little girl, but that wasn't enough for me. I wanted to be perfect.

The barrier to perfection seemed to be the word "kitchen." I was very good at spelling, but just couldn't seem to master "kitchen." (My husband Joel says this was a portent of things to come; I have hundreds of cook books but throughout my life I have avoided any serious attempts at cooking. Joel is fond of recounting how many delicious meals he has read.)

When the spelling test came, I was prepared. In my left hand, in the crook of a finger, I had a tiny piece of paper with kitchen on it. I felt I was safe; my seat was in the fourth row, over by the bulletin board. No one would notice.

When I reached the crucial point on the test, I furtively looked down at my left hand, wrote down "kitchen" (correctly) and was able to achieve perfection at last.

Until I looked up. There was Miss Huff, my teacher, looking me right in the eye.

(Continued)

(Continued)

She walked to my desk. She leaned down close. "Betty Faye," she whispered, "I saw you cheating. Please see me at recess."

My life was over. Not only was I not perfect, I wasn't even a good girl anymore. The few minutes until recess were the longest minutes in my life.

After everyone else had trooped out, Miss Huff called me to her desk. I was in tears. "What are you going to do to me?" I wasn't in any position to think clearly, but it wouldn't have surprised me if the sheriff had walked in.

Miss Huff just took my hands and looked me right in the eye. She was serious, talking to me (I realize now) as a child far beyond my years.

"Betty Faye," she said, "Don't you know you're smart? You don't need to cheat." She said it again for emphasis. "You're smart. You don't need to cheat."

She saved my life.

I think this experience was what propelled me into a lifelong career of teaching and was ultimately what drove my commitment to promote excellence and integrity at all levels of the educational spectrum. It was what inspired my life goal of passing this commitment on to others. This saint of a woman, teaching in a tiny school in rural Kentucky, chose to use my mistake, not to make an example of me by punishing me, but by teaching me that the test of character is how you behave even when no one is looking.

Changing Perspective: Bigger Than We Are

There are a plethora of causes and creeds in the world today that call to people to look beyond themselves; we are not championing any one or group of those. What we are saying is that if you want your commitment to be sustainable, if you want to enroll others into engaging with you in achieving your goal, you will want to be committed to something bigger than you are. You may be committed to changing the way students are taught in your community, or you may be inspiring fourth grade girls to respect their character; your choice, but make it bigger than you are.

And enrolling others is critical. If you are flying on your own, it will be a short flight. We are a social species; we bring different strengths and talents to the table; we accomplish our most meaningful and important things as teams and communities.

The Pole Vault and the Decathlon Life

It is intriguing to us that when performing the pole vault, the athlete looks first to the sky, then twists and looks down the pole— their contact with the earth—to the ground. Then they gently push that pole, their last structure of support, of earthly contact, from their grasp. They are flying free, but they are facing toward the ground, toward the arena, toward the physical reality.

The pole vault reminds us that what is possible is a change in perspective, a change in orientation, a change in focus. Your perspective changes first from the mundane to the wonderful; from the present to the future. You rise into the future to look from the perspective of the future, where all is possible. This is where you create your vision, at the apex of your vault; this is where you begin to craft the rest of your life.

Then you turn, elegantly, athletically, to look into the "groundedness" of the present, not being seduced by the allure of the future. You turn to plan out what can be done, what needs to be done, what you can do; and even more, what you can do if you enroll others in your perspective, orientation, and commitment.

And this is a place where you can learn from your experience of enrolling your advisory board.

Enrolling Your Advisory Board – And Beyond

When you began your Decathlon Life and were enrolling your board members, you had to become *clear about what you were committed to* or you weren't going to enroll anybody.

Your board members became enrolled because they sensed your commitment, your dream, your vision, your spirit.

Your inspiration.

They became enrolled (this was something they did on their own, not something you "did to them") because *you* were inspired by your vision, your commitment. Some part of them recognized that something of value was being offered to them and they wanted to be part of what you were up to. They were inspired because you were inspired, and they wanted to have some of that.

That can be your pattern, your template.

If you want to change things in the world, expand your boundaries, create a bigger future, show people what inspires you. Enroll them in your dream.

It may give you your first glimpse, or perhaps a clearer view, of what you came to do.

THE 1500 METERS

CHAPTER 15

THE 1500 METERS

Celebration

Don't Forget the Party!

What a ride! Would you have thought that it would all turn out like this? Did you have any idea you would learn so much, hate it so much, or love it so much?

Did you anticipate meeting so many great people?

Let's have a party! Let's get everybody together!

Let's run together through the neighborhood for a mile or so...say, about 1500 Meters?

The 1500 meters is the last event on the decathlon schedule. Called the "Metric Mile," it is actually 0.93 miles in length, 100 meters less than four laps of the 400 meter track. It is the "glamour" middle distance run of track and field competition.

It is also the most back-breaking event of the decathlon.

The decathlon competition, held over two twelve or thirteen hour days, is both exhausting and exhilarating. It can wear competitors out while it is inspiring them and motivating them to accomplish things they didn't know they had in them.

In other words, it is a lot like life.

Virtually none of the decathletes are world-class middle distance runners; if their resume includes a dominant event it is almost a lock that it will not be the 1500 meters.

The event is traditionally scheduled at 9:00 p.m. or later at the end of the second day of intense athletic competition and energy-sapping physical exertion. The first event each day is routinely scheduled to begin at about 9:00 a.m.; five events are completed each day for the total of ten events. The tenth, concluding event on the second day is always the 1500 meters. You can count on the fact that the competitors will be running on adrenalin.

In unguarded moments, decathlon competitors will say things like "I was doing okay until the 1500 meters, but that just killed me." It is an awfully long and exhausting two days.

Celebration? Are You Kidding Me?

A tough event, at the end of an exhausting two days of competition, and even worse, an event that no one is all that good at. Where's the fun, where's the celebration in that?

To begin to answer that question, let's look at the contrast between the Opening Ceremonies and the Closing Ceremonies in an Olympic Games.

The Opening Ceremonies

The traditional Opening Ceremonies include the Parade of Athletes, with teams of "uniformed" athletes marching into the stadium behind their country's flag. It is all very formal; the choice of flag bearer is of great importance, as is the opportunity to express national pride and cultural mores in the selection of the clothing worn by the athletes; sometimes modern and dashing,  sometimes very traditional. Each team's sequential position in the march comes according to the alphabetical order of the name of their country, except that Greece, the original home of the Olympic Games, always leads the march and the host nation always enters the stadium last.

All very official, all very formal. We are about to engage in serious international competition here, people, and there is a lot of tradition and protocol to pay homage to.

The Closing Ceremonies

Then a couple of weeks later, the competition is over and everything changes. The flag bearers march in, but no athletes are behind them. The bearers carry their flags to their designated area and wait. The crowd waits as well. Then the athletes come in.

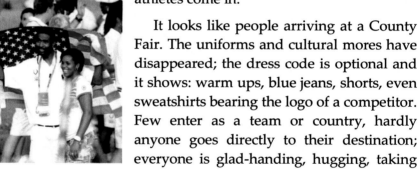

It looks like people arriving at a County Fair. The uniforms and cultural mores have disappeared; the dress code is optional and it shows: warm ups, blue jeans, shorts, even sweatshirts bearing the logo of a competitor. Few enter as a team or country, hardly anyone goes directly to their destination; everyone is glad-handing, hugging, taking pictures and having their picture taken, and having a ball. Some wear medals, most don't; it doesn't matter. Nobody stands on protocol; everybody is among friends.

It's a celebration.

It is a gathering of athletes representing all manner of sports, all countries and cultures, all languages. It doesn't matter. All are fierce competitors, the world's best, engaging in what is perhaps the peak experience of their lives, but tonight nobody is keeping score. Tonight nobody is trying to win anything. It is not outrageous to imagine that this is what it was like at the end of the games back in ancient Greece.

It is magic.

The 1500 Meters as a Celebration

So far, we know two things about the 1500 meters: it is always the last event on the schedule, coming on the evening of the second day, and history says that none of the competitors are dominant middle distance runners. There are two other characteristics, however, that give the 1500 meters its unique claim to celebration:

- The competitor who is ahead in the point totals going into the 1500 meters has an excellent chance to hold his lead if he just *completes* the event; the point spread between the winner and the last place finisher in the 1500 meters rarely allows any challenger to suddenly come from behind and take the overall point total lead. There are exceptions, but the 1500 meters is a race for endurance, for completion, for avoiding disaster, not for dominating or embarrassing the field.

- Amazingly enough, the 1500 meters is the *only event* of the decathlon where all of the decathletes are on the track together *at the same time.*

This last observation is significant. As you recall, a decathlete's performance against the clock or the tape measure earns them a certain number of points; at the end of the two days, the winner is the one with the greatest cumulative number of points.

During the two days, however, the running events are run in *heats.* Six or eight decathletes will run the 110 meter hurdles or the 100 meters dash or the 400 meters against each other and their individual times will be recorded and scored; then six or eight more will repeat the process in another heat. The weights and jumps are, of course, individually performed; only one competitor at a time can pole vault or put the shot, and an individual's jumps or throws for an event can sometimes stretch on for two or more hours.

But the 1500 meters sees all the athletes on the track together, at the same time, for the first time in two days. And chances are, no one is going to run away with the event. Plus, it is the end of a long, exhausting competition that is finally coming to an end.

What a great time for a celebration!

Can you see the parallels with the Closing Ceremonies? The competitors have become compatriots. There is only one gold medal winner, but all on the track have engaged, have given their all, and have contributed their prodigious gifts. These are the best athletes in the world who have just spent an exhausting two days trying to perform better than they have ever performed in their lives and virtually all of them have accomplished just that.

They are members of a very exclusive fraternity; they are joined together in a sort of global oneness of excellence. They have experienced triumphs and shared experiences and created memories that will last the rest of their lives. And it is all about to be over.

Now they are going for a final run together through the neighborhood.

It's a celebration!

Betty Does Celebration

From Bill:

Betty Siegel is no stranger to celebration, to ceremony, to festive occasions; she has been the commencement speaker at countless graduation ceremonies, both at her own university and at many others; in addition, she has received scores of awards around the world and has been awarded eight honorary doctoral degrees. I thought she would have a plethora of stories about these ceremonies and celebrations but in typical Betty style she chose to relate one from years ago when she was a university professor:

(Continued)

(Continued)

I was the first woman hired as a professor into a large department at the University of Florida, one woman and thirty-five men. As a trend setter, however, I didn't set an instantaneous trend; it was years before they hired their second female professor. By that time, I had decided to get the men's attention.

When a department hired a new professor, it was traditional for the University to treat all of the department's professors to a steak dinner to welcome the newcomer on board. This celebration was where I decided to make my move.

After elaborate plotting and preparations, the new lady professor and I arrived at the dinner dressed in our husbands' clothes (suit, dress shirt, tie, and enormous shoes) and sporting huge cigars. We had decided to come as "two of the boys."

After the other professors finished laughing at two crazy ladies (and, on reflection, at themselves), they realized that one of the traditions of a storied institution had been modernized. It was a steak dinner celebration for the history books, and along the way all of us had expanded our boundaries, once and forever. Change had begun.

Betty says that in that department, they still talk about "remember when those two women dressed up like men..." That's the part she likes best.

Celebrating Your Decathlon Life

So you have completed your project, engaged in your own unique version of the Decathlon Life, and accomplished what you committed to do. The experience might have taken some twists and turns, starts and stops, even major redesigns, but you have stayed the course. It is time for a celebration!

Lots of people probably had a hand in your success, some you don't even know about. Certainly your advisory board and your family deserve some applause. The world is a better place for those who participated with you and perhaps for some others who benefitted from what you accomplished. They will want to celebrate with you, in whatever way they choose.

The origin of the word "celebration" is the Latin word *celebratus*, which curiously enough meant "to frequent." Perhaps when languages were coming into being, tribal or cultural activities that occurred frequently became referred to by the term "celebration," and over the years the word took on its modern meaning of a ceremony or festival.

We are not speaking of a celebration just as an event—"We will meet down at the City Park at one p.m. Saturday and eat hot dogs and drink beer"—we are speaking of celebration as a human declaration, as an attitude; we are grateful for the gift of life, for relationships that nurture and inspire us, for opportunities to express who we are that fulfill us.

It is this expression of gratitude that calls to us. In today's world, far too much discussion centers around what our rights are, what we are entitled to, what our social position or wealth or membership or heritage or citizenship gives us a right to claim as ours.

How refreshing to turn instead to celebrating because we have been given a gift. *Grace* has been defined as *unmerited favor*, and all of us can remember times in our lives when we received a generous portion of grace. One elderly comedian talks of being grateful that, once again this morning, he woke up "on the right side of the grass."

So celebrate, early and often. We are winners once again!

Your Friends the Celebrities

The word "celebrity" originally meant "in the state of being celebrated."

We assert that when we celebrate a friend or a teammate, when we recognize, acknowledge, and express our gratitude for their contribution and support, we anoint them as celebrities.

Who would dare to challenge our authority to do this?

We hereby solemnly grant this authority to you. Celebrate your team, your advisory board, your family, your supporters, and anyone else who should be celebrated. Declare them to be celebrities.

Surround yourself with celebrities!

Making It Real

Take one more step for closure, to plant your journey in your memory. I was there, so were all of you; we created a better future than would have occurred without us.

Mark this time, this special expression of your unique craftsmanship, this moment when you exceeded your previous best, when you stood on the medal stand with the spirits of the Olympians of ancient Greece and the decathletes of today.

When you celebrated your own Decathlon Life.

Paint in the other eye of your Daruma!

And, umm…

What's next?

EPILOGUE

THE BLACK HORSE
AND THE DECATHLON LIFE

In ancient mythology, horses of three colors—white, red, and black—were often used as symbols for three stages in a human's life: childhood, the producing years and old age. Societal expectations and biases can cloud the distinctions of what each stage brings, however; so we offer our Decathlon Life version:

The rider of the Black Horse is often surprised to find themselves in the saddle. The transition from the Red Horse to the Black Horse is subtle, and is marked by a movement from *passion* to *inclusion*—as in, you do not agree with the opinion being voiced, because it is clearly in opposition to your opinion—but you are willing to include it. It is as though you are taking a picture of your extended family, and you suggest to your nutty Uncle Frank that he step into the picture, even though he is not your favorite relative. You include him in the picture because, well, it doesn't hurt you, and he is a member of the family.

Inclusion is powerful. Inclusion causes you to extend your boundaries. You may not like anything about Uncle Frank, but Aunt Edith married him, so he must have some redeeming qualities. And a voice in the back of your head whispers that there may be some of the family who would have left you out.

The Red Horse, on the other hand, is about passion, finding what you believe in and defending it. It is not about including but about *excluding* all that keeps you from your quest, all that distracts you from finding your Grail. The Red Horse can lead you to personal fulfillment that people literally will die for; there is nothing quite like the ride on the Red Horse.

Except, perhaps, when you find yourself ambling serenely along—on a Black Horse?

How did that happen?

Perhaps the answer lies in one of the "whys" behind this three-color trifecta of our experience of life. In understanding our human journey, for example, the White, Red, and Black horses can be metaphors for the ways in which we deal with *trust*—and like inclusion, trust is a very powerful concept.

Many dictionaries defining trust speak about "placing confidence" in someone or something, "relying on," "expecting," without fear or misgiving. Trust almost always requires two or more players (we will speak about the exception in a moment). There are probably as many versions of trust as there are human beings, but three things are clear: trust is important, it is not easily earned, and it is much more easily lost.

The symbolic horses are directly connected to our life experiences of trust:

- The White Horse, which brings *innocence*, is a symbol of our childhood. When we ride the White Horse, we learn to *trust other people*: our parents, later our teachers and perhaps our coaches, some of our friends and maybe a few others. We learn to do as we are told because we have confidence that others are giving us good instructions. If we find that this trust is misplaced, this is good training also and we learn to be discerning when we trust others. If we find that we cannot find anyone trustworthy (literally, worthy of our trust) during our ride on the White Horse, that can force us into a premature and risky switch to the Red Horse.

- The Red Horse, which brings *passion*, is a symbol of the productive and creative period of our life, beginning in adolescence and continuing through our "earning years." When we ride the Red Horse, we are learning to *trust ourselves*. This is the one exception that we spoke of earlier, the time when there is only one player in the game. We are giving ourselves a tryout to see if we can be trusted; we are testing different behaviors, different passions, and different priorities. Sometimes these tryouts can last for years or even decades; it is never too late to grow up to be who you wanted to be. We continue to trust others, of course, as we did while riding the White Horse, but we have added the new and crucial dimension of learning to trust ourselves.

- The Black Horse, which brings *wisdom*, is a symbol of our "crowning" years when we are free from earning our daily bread and can focus on what is meaningful. When we ride the Black Horse, we learn to *trust something larger than we are*. We may trust God, or nature, or freedom, or a more perfect society, or whatever else we are willing to align ourselves with, but we are acknowledging that we are not the center of all existence, and that other opinions and traditions and authorities may in fact have some merit. This could be called inclusion in action. We trust others, and ourselves, as before, but we sense that something more, something profound, has arrived on stage. We find ourselves astride the Black Horse.

The Black Horse is all about judgment as opposed to passion; moderation as an alternative to boldness. Michael Goldberg, writing of Homer's *Odyssey*[4], described the Cyclops as a creature of primitive energy, unsophisticated, aggressive, passionate; a poster child for the rider of the Red Horse. The Cyclops, however, had only one eye—Homer was illustrating that this primitive energy lacked *perspective*.

And this is what the Black Horse rider has gained: perspective. The ability to look at other alternatives, to adjust beliefs and positions, to *include* the valuable ideas and contributions of others— even those you fundamentally disagree with. Even Uncle Frank.

And Goldberg also speaks of Odysseus maintaining, throughout his decade-long journey, a vision of Ithaca, of *home*. The rider of the Black Horse comes to sense that this planet, this life, may not be our true home, and this gives a further measure of perspective and trust; trust in something beyond symbols, beyond metaphors, beyond time and space, beyond mere human being.

Riding the Black Horse is almost certain to be one of your experiences of living the Decathlon Life. We wish you a long and fulfilling ride.

---

[4] Michael Goldberg, *Travels With Odysseus* (Circe's Island Press, 2006).

APPENDIX

STAYING CONNECTED

> Two caterpillars were crawling along a tree branch one day when a butterfly flew overhead. One caterpillar said to the other, "You will never get me up in one of those things."
>
> — Robert Holden, *Shift Happens*

It occurred to us that the individual participants of the Decathlon Life might want to have a relatively straightforward way to communicate with each other, or with the authors, now that their younger Advisory Board members have taught them the intricacies of electronic communication. To that end, we have established a website imaginatively titled thedecathlonlife.com. We think you will like it.

The world is always changing, but today it seems to be changing at a faster pace. The problem with books like this one is that they are one-and-done; there is no practical way to "update" them to include new ideas and new approaches. A website, however, can be changed easily and effectively; new information can be added, new priorities can be emphasized, new resources can be identified and utilized. The possibilities are limitless.

The Design of the Website

We would like to describe the website to you but we actually don't know what it will look like by the time you read this. That is the beauty of flexibility and change. However, here are the things we want the website to provide in the long term:

- The site will contain new material that is relevant to many or all of the chapters of the book. We are constantly thinking of additional angles on the event metaphors; we want to pass those on to you. In addition, as we talk to people who read the book we will better understand the challenges that you are facing in engaging in the Decathlon Life and we will be able to pass on the insight and wisdom of your fellow participants. We will post these insights, observations, and experiences on the website, always keeping your privacy secure.

- We will post links to other resources on the internet: articles you might want to read, news that may affect you, reviews of movies, or books you might be interested in. There's a lot of information out there and you can pick and choose from some of the things we have come across

- We may post links to short videos that we find interesting, such as interviews with interesting people, or lessons on how to high jump or pole vault for the *really* engaged.

- We will continue to look at other opportunities that show up as things in the world change; resources for you that we can't even guess at today.

We hope you'll join us. Even if you've sworn that they'll never get you up in one of those things.

Just get one of your grandkids to get you started.

thedecathlonlife.com

ABOUT THE AUTHORS

Dr. Betty Siegel is President Emeritus of Kennesaw State University; she retired in 2006 after twenty-five years as President. She was the first woman to head a unit in the University System of Georgia and during her term KSU grew from an enrollment of 4,000 to 18,000 students. Betty has spoken on leadership and delivered keynote addresses at conferences and conclaves in all fifty states and eleven foreign countries and this endeavor continues to this day. Betty and her husband Joel reside in a suburb of Atlanta. And yes, she is famous for the eyeglasses.

Bill Dyke worked as an industrial engineer and manufacturing manager with Procter & Gamble, as a computer system salesman and sales executive with IBM and as an independent marketing systems and management development consultant serving clients such as AT&T, Canadian National Railroad, Coopers & Lybrand, IBM, Neiman Marcus and REI. He and his wife Jan reside in a suburb of Atlanta. The last time he jumped a hurdle was at the age of 60 and he was successful. To a degree.

PICTURE CREDITS

The organizations or individual photographers listed below own all rights to the photographs used in this book. All photos are courtesy of Shutterstock.com unless otherwise noted below.